BIRTH
OF A
UNICORN

Six Basic Steps to Success

Heather Wilde

SUNBURY
PRESS
Mechanicsburg, PA USA

Published by Sunbury Press, Inc.
Mechanicsburg, Pennsylvania

www.sunburypress.com

For information about special discounts for bulk purchases, please contact Sunbury Press Orders Dept. at (855) 338-8359 or orders@sunburypress.com.

To request one of our authors for speaking engagements or book signings, please contact Sunbury Press Publicity Dept. at publicity@sunburypress.com.

FIRST SUNBURY PRESS EDITION: November 2020

Set in Adobe Garamond | Interior design by Crystal Devine | Cover by Christina Clemente | Edited by Abigail Henson.

Publisher's Cataloging-in-Publication Data
Names: Wilde, Heather, author.
Title: Birth of a unicorn / Heather Wilde.
Description: First hardcover edition. | Mechanicsburg, PA : Sunbury Press, 2020.
Summary: A young female entrepreneur shares her methods for success in both business and life.
Identifiers: ISBN 978-1-620063-34-7 (hardcover).
Subjects: BUSINESS & ECONOMICS / Entrepreneurship | BUSINESS & ECONOMICS / Personal Success | BUSINESS & ECONOMICS / Women in Business | SELF-HELP / Personal Growth / Happiness.

Product of the United States of America
0 1 1 2 3 5 8 13 21 34 55

Continue the Enlightenment!

FOR SUSAN

It is so shocking to find out how many people do not believe that they can learn, and how many more believe learning to be difficult.

—FRANK HERBERT

Contents

Foreword | ix

Introduction | 1

CHAPTERS

  1. Beginnings | 5

  2. Uncertainty | 18

  3. Significance | 41

  4. Love & Connection | 55

  5. Contribution | 66

  6. Growth | 85

  7. Certainty | 99

  8. Rinse & Repeat | 123

  9. Epilogue | 137

  10. Now What? | 140

Acknowledgments | 144

About the Author | 146

Foreword

I FIRST MET Heather in the hot Nevada summer of 2015, when Heather was working with Mark Rowland and Tony Hsieh in RO-Ceteer. ROCeteer was seeding investment in my startup, Fingerprint for Success.

In Fingerprint for Success, I was commercializing my life's work from being one of the earliest professional coaches in the world. By then, I had published several handbooks on professional coaching, trained executive, business, and personal coaches in 60 countries, and had personally coached 1000+ founders, including eight unicorn and startup founders who achieved multi-hundred-million dollar exits and multi-billion dollar IPOs. I had just completed a world-first peer-reviewed study on the motivations of the world's most successful founders.

Heather did not know it at the time, but she had a big reputation to live up to. I had learned from those who work closely with her that she was like no other they had worked with. Heather was whip-smart and genius-like, able to achieve in minutes what would take anybody else, well, days.

Over these years, Heather has far exceeded her reputation, not only through her abilities and achievements but by her kind hospitality and deep, genuine desire to help and serve others.

In her short but rich and diverse life, Heather has experienced and achieved more than folk double her age. Her genuine heart for contribution, her unique experiences, and original storytelling make Heather a bona fide force for good. Especially so if you have been fortunate to have made it to the top of Heather's waitlist, and she has been your advisor, coach, speaker, or mentor.

Reading *Birth of a Unicorn* will take you on a never-before-published, insider's tale of a note-taking app's startup journey from a couple of thousand users to more than 225 million users worldwide. A startup journey of becoming the world's most used note-taking app.

You will be entertained as you travel along with Heather's unique role in the growth of Evernote. You will discover unique business strategies and high-impact lessons that you can apply to your own startup journey and big life goals.

While Heather's business takeaways have a multiplying power to positively change your career or business, in *Birth of a Unicorn* you will also be inspired and facilitated to design a life that serves your unique passions and life purpose. You will be invited to a life that flames your deep psychological, motivational needs.

Heather uses the impactful Six Human Needs motivational framework for transparently unpacking the design of her own life, her decisions, and her learnings. Heather provides you with a simple and impactful tool for identifying your own motivational needs and many pragmatic recommendations for how to meet these needs.

Birth of a Unicorn is a gift like no other from Heather, to be savored one page at a time.

Enjoy!

Michelle Duval

Introduction

All of us have to learn how to invent our lives, make them up, imagine them. We need to be taught these skills; we need guides to show us how. If we don't, our lives get made up for us by other people.

—URSULA K. LE GUIN,
THE WAVE IN THE MIND

ERICH FROMM said, "The quest for certainty blocks the search for meaning. Uncertainty is the very condition to impel man to unfold his powers."

Many fear the uncertawinty of the future. The constant anxiety that many people feel is often rooted in fear: fear of the unknown. Not many people are willing to go or even take the first step on a path without knowing where they go or how they will get there. Obtaining success and being happy is more comfortable to talk about than it is to achieve, for achieving those goals requires a journey. Winston Churchill said, "Success is not final, failure is not fatal: it is the courage to continue that counts."

It is possible to live your life without being happy and content and to look back on it and wonder what happened to your dreams and goals. Questions such as, "Where did I go wrong?" and "What could I have done differently?" may flood your mind. These are questions that often remain unanswered. I want to give you the answers, but before I do, let me introduce you to my story because I am going to weave the solutions throughout this book.

There are only two things in life that are certain—taxes and death, and there is no guarantee for anything else in our lives. When you stop to think about this, you will come to terms with two things: you cannot avoid taking risks and making choices since life is filled with uncertainty. The truth is that we do not learn to avoid the unknown; instead, we adapt and learn to deal with things as they come.

We need to get to that place where we learn to accept all kinds of ambiguities and recognize that acceptance is a vital step in growth. Learning to accept uncertainty is the only logical thing we can do to enjoy life.

The core of my coaching methods rests on six basic needs for humanity:

- Uncertainty (or Variety)
- Significance
- Love/Connection
- Growth
- Contribution
- Certainty

In this guide, we will explore all six basic needs. From these six, we all have at least one basic need, which reflects our inner selves; it is the real core of identity that defines us—that part of us that seeks happiness. We all search for true contentment and inner peace, and without them, there is emptiness. My quest for happiness is an adventure, and I invite you to share my experiences as I recount the good and the bad of my journey to success.

Of the six basic needs, I have chosen to begin my tale with Uncertainty as this is the starting point for most. We face many decisions in life, and very seldom do we know where our choices will take us. We flip a coin and hope for the best, force ourselves to remain optimistic, and every so often, that hope is the only thing we have. It is difficult to ignore those very annoying voices in the back of our head telling us to remain in our comfort zones and to venture away from them.

It seldom helps to hear the horror stories of others who have faced the "Uncertainty Demon" and lost, but our outcome will never be determined by another's experience. In other words, you can never truly predict your end even with all the knowledge you may have acquired. Unless you take the journey, you will never know what it entails or where it will lead you. I know this well.

It took me a while to achieve my success; it certainly did not happen overnight. My journey is the culmination of a series of events that led me to victory. I desire to reveal truthfully how I got where I am. My life, my journey, is a testament that says you can achieve whatever you want when you set your mind to it. I did it; so can you.

1.
Beginnings

RITUALS

I used to have a morning ritual.

Each morning, I would hit the snooze alarm a few times, carefully calculating each additional seven minutes of rest, then wake up and turn on the television to the local news. I would sleepily gather my clothes for the day, then meander into the shower. Like clockwork, I would always be out of the shower by 8:25 A.M., ready to brush my hair, watch the news, get dressed, and go to work—so I could roll into the office by 9:00 A.M..

This particular Tuesday started the same as always.

"Shorty came in, and she caught me red-handed . . ." Snooze.

"I-iiiiiiii want to thannnnnnk you . . ." Snooze.

"I'm a Survivor, ain't gonna . . ." Snooze!

After the third song, I woke up, a bit groggy, but no worse for wear. On came the television.

"Traffic on I-93 SB is flowing well into the city . . ." It was an average day.

I absent-mindedly grabbed my towel and headed for the shower. A few blissful minutes later, I emerged, dripping and ready to detangle my hair, which took a while, so I grabbed my hairbrush and sat on my bed in front of the TV.

They were talking about normal morning news things when suddenly, there was a bright red "Breaking News" banner.

An aircraft of unknown size or origin had crashed into the World Trade Center. There was no other information available.

I dropped the brush.

I looked at the clock. It was 8:45 A.M.

I grabbed the phone.

I was a newlywed—not yet married a year. My husband Leon was a charter pilot who flew for the military.

We had a ritual. Every night, before we went to bed, he would call me from wherever he was, and tell me where he would be flying the next day. He would go over his route with me, in detail, so newlywed me would not have to worry. I could look at the clock and know that he was over Arkansas, or Richmond, or New York City.

He would take me flying with him, so I would get to know the exact patterns of his flights, where he would need to turn, and where things could go wrong.

That Monday night, he had gone over with me that he would be flying from Maryland to New York, with a flight pattern over Manhattan that involved flying straight toward the Twin Towers—so close you could feel the wind disturbance from them—and then turning around the city.

We had flown this route together only a few weeks prior on Labor Day Weekend. The winds had been so bad we cracked the windshield of our rental plane.

For this flight, the time he would be over Manhattan was 8:45 A.M.

I was so tired and selfishly distracted that Monday night, I wanted to get off the phone quickly. I cannot even remember if I said I love you.

Staring at the TV, with color drained from my face, I reached over to my nightstand and grabbed my phone. I called his cell phone, but all circuits were busy, and I could not get through. I called the flight dispatcher, and they could not give me any information either. I called the airport—nothing.

I called the place where he was staying to find out if he had gone to work that morning. Yes, he had.

I called the local news station to find out if they knew anything. They hung up on me, telling me they needed to keep the lines clear for emergency reports.

I called everyone I knew that might be able to help me find answers. Did the man I love pilot the plane that had crashed into the tower?

When the other plane crashed soon after, I wondered if the man I love was responsible for causing two planes to crash?

And when the towers fell, I questioned if the man I love caused all those people to die?

While it seems ancient history now, it was many hours before the news reports changed from "small plane" or "unidentified aircraft" to "coordinated terrorist attack." By then, I had been in a heightened state of panic for hours. This intense emotion, stress, and feeling of helplessness had locked itself into my brain—forever.

Later that evening, around 5 P.M., Leon called. They grounded him from flying that morning, and since his base had been on lockdown, no one was allowed to call out.

When I found out that he was alive and his flight had been grounded just before the first attack, when all communication lines went down, something inside me changed. I felt a great loss for the victims and their loved ones. Even after knowing the truth, a part of me could not remove the initial misplaced guilt that it was somehow his plane that started it all. That day started me into a grief spiral that I could not escape.

Due to his unique position, he was one of the few civilian pilots who had clearance to fly over the city in the days following, which meant that I did not get to see him for another few weeks.

When he finally returned home, the woman that awaited him was a stranger. The jovial, bubbly, spoiled girl-child he had married was gone, replaced by a guarded and sad young woman. I was fearful of his going away to fly. I was uncertain of the future.

SACRIFICE

Leon and I were married in December 2000. We had an unconventional marriage—reminiscent of military deployment. He was an airline pilot, and for the first two years of our marriage, we lived apart because his job based him in Richmond, VA—600 miles away from mine, in Boston, MA. We did not see each other much, maybe every other weekend for a day or less. As we were just starting our lives together, we barely had the money for gas, much less a plane ticket; this relegated us to seeing each other only when he could hop a flight in the jump-seat of a plane heading somewhere north.

To cope with my absence, Leon got a cat to help pass the lonely nights. He named the cat Bastian after a character in one of my favorite books, *The Neverending Story*, and he would spend hours talking to the cat. It was not long until Bastian was as much a member of the family as I was.

After 9/11, things changed. I stayed home, transfixed by the images of destruction in New York. I watched the footage on repeat. Hours would pass, and I would continue to view all the angles and listen to the stories. I stopped eating—all I could do was cry.

My group of friends in Boston were all from New York City, and all of us were affected similarly. Since one of the aircraft departed Boston, a pall hung over the city. There was a melancholy feel to everything—and while I imagine everyone in the country was grieving, I could not see a way out.

Eventually, I decided that I needed to break the cycle. I turned wholeheartedly to my work with renewed vigor. I was now often the first to arrive and last to leave. I volunteered for night and weekend shifts, which no one else wanted. I became the perfect employee.

I have always been a driven person, someone who works hard and has goals I want to achieve. However, after the towers fell in New York, Leon saw that I was in a crisis. To move past my depression, I needed my husband.

He took stock of the situation and realized that he could not take me away from the one thing that was holding me together—my work. He would have to give up his dreams of flying to support me emotionally, help me to get better, and, ultimately, help me to succeed.

Unlike most other jobs, where a transition from one company to another means upward career mobility, in the airline industry, a pilot must start at the bottom rung of the ladder at each new employer. The years he dedicated to getting better schedules, higher pay, and better aircraft were suddenly in his rear-view mirror because of his love for me. That was a bold move on his part. He sacrificed his entire career for me in one moment. At the time, I did not even recognize it—I could not because I was swirling in the depths of depression. The only way out was for someone else to pull me forward.

VANITY METRICS

When I was finally emotionally ready to start to look at the world around me again, I found that things had changed dramatically.

I had been working at a boutique game studio near Boston, MA since 1999. We had released some cult-favorite games designed for online play. There was only one catch—after 9/11, people were not in the mood to play games anymore.

For a month or so after the attack, people would log in to the server for our main game and sit in the chat area, not playing any games—they would go in and start talking to each other. We noticed this trend spread to our other games as well. Overnight, we had become a group therapy chatroom service.

Any profits we had made selling expansion packs and sets dried up right away. We had to do something.

I had an idea to try to turn things around. I had a theory that if I could shift the mood of the conversation, people would start playing again. Our latest release was a Star Trek game, so I pulled aside our CEO, Shawn Broderick, and asked him if I could add a mini-game in the chatroom.

My idea was simple: I wanted to write a trivia bot that would ask questions (mostly Star Trek, but some other Sci-Fi as well) and keep cumulative and all-time scores. I wanted the all-time scores to be appended (so people could just keep getting insane amounts over time), and there to be 3-question rounds so people could win prizes that would be useful within the game.

At the time, this was revolutionary. There was no "online" to speak of, and multiplayer games were barely a blip.

Shawn said, "Sounds good." He was a man of few words, so this was high praise.

I pulled aside a co-worker, and we started working on it immediately. We were immersed in Star Trek history and other books for a week to get a list of over 5000 questions and answers to load into the system. Ten days later, we loaded it into the system, and I announced it on our forums, our website, and in our newsletter. I even cross-posted it with our other game that was sci-fi related, in hopes that the fuss would make people register for our Star Trek game.

It worked.

Within one day, the game came back to life. Before the Trivia Bot, there had been 1-5 people logged in at any one time. Afterward, we had 30-40 at any given time (and this was still when you needed to buy a modem and tie up a phone line to reach the internet). They loved every minute of it. They were fighting to be the first to type in the answers. They had macros to answer the questions the fastest. One question had been entered incorrectly into the database—the answer came before the question—and this became one of the more popular 'questions,' as everyone raced to type in:

"What popular movie series is based around a time machine powered by a flux capacitor?"

Someone even created a flash-based website and a set of memes for the Trivia Bot.

I had struck community gold!

It was awesome, until we noticed the trends.

People still were not playing the *actual* game. They were not buying sets or pieces. They only registered accounts just to login and play trivia, and then sat on our servers for hours—sometimes days—at a time to do it.

As my friend Phil Libin likes to say, "feedback is good for telling you what you're doing wrong, but a terrible indicator of anything else."

And boy, did we get feedback. We had a lot of it, from all sides—and it was all encouraging. Customers and journalists alike told us how great we were doing. They gushed at how excellent our products were.

On a personal note, my colleagues hailed me as a fantastic, resourceful wunderkind. Every day I was told I was changing the world of online games and making an impact. It seems such an easy thing to say in hindsight—people were just polite, or they were encouraging us out of love, or duty, or friendship. But, honestly—that is useless in business.

We needed to know what our faults were to correct them, and be better, do better, make the best product. For every one person who has an issue and voices it, there are at least ten times that many who do not bother to speak up.

Since we were not tracking the right metrics, we started to focus on the outliers, the complainers—the bad reviews, mainly—to figure out what was wrong and see if we could salvage it. We also decided to hold a meeting where we were brainstorming ways to monetize the new traffic we were getting. The people were out there; we just had to figure out how to convert them.

While we convened in a conference room, there was a knock on the door. Shawn peeked his head in, "Hey, Heather, can I borrow you for a sec?"

We walked over to his office, and he sat me down. There were papers on his desk that he was shuffling a bit nervously.

"I'm sorry to have to tell you this, but headquarters is closing us down."

He explained that our parent company was shuttering companies that were not profitable or did not align with their current goals. He did not elaborate on which we were, but it was apparent.

He shook my hand and walked me to my desk, then went back to the meeting room and proceeded to tell everyone else, one by one.

As I drove home that day along I-95, I could not help but notice how many of the buildings that had been bustling just a year ago were now vacant and dark. There were for-rent and for-sale signs everywhere.

I felt a deep sense of shame on that drive, having to go home and tell my husband that I had lost my job—after he gave everything up for me.

PINBALL WIZARDS

I had just gotten my groove back, and suddenly I was floundering again.

When the economy collapsed, the world turned overnight, and the impact I had made turned out to be a resounding "THUD." It did not make any sense. We had been going to change the world—everyone was on board! So why did they abandon us? If we were so amazing, why did we not survive? If everything was as amazing as everyone had been telling us—why were we out of jobs?

My nascent marriage already was not on the steadiest footing, and now I had lost my income. With no one supporting us, one of us needed to find a job quickly.

Leon had decided to use his time in Boston to go back to school for another college degree. When this happened, he started putting in calls at airlines to see if anyone was hiring, but after 9/11, no one was. He did have an offer to join the Air National Reserve, but I was still too emotionally fragile to let him go. That became a dead end—and a sore point.

Thankfully, I did not have to wait for long. An acquaintance of mine, Phil Libin, was thinking of starting a new company. As a Russian immigrant who grew up in New York City, he had also been deeply affected by the events of 9/11. He wanted to create a company based around the idea that the only people who can get into something like an airline cockpit should be authorized to be there.

"Because, you know—if there is any way I can stop this from happening again, I'm going to do it. Uh. Hmm. Do you think you can maybe help me with that?"

Phil had a shy, questioning look on his face—almost like he was looking for approval. The tone of voice he used was gentle and quiet, belying the deep passion he felt for this project. I felt that connection—the need he was trying to fill. I just did not know how I would be able to help.

"What do you want me to do?" I asked.

"Oh, I don't know," he said, swatting the air and shaking his head. "We'll figure it out. You're resourceful, right? I need people who believe in this and are willing to work."

Having nothing better to do at the time, I said, "Sure, why not."

I needed to get out of the house, and this fitted the bill.

Initially, we were trying to find our footing as a company. We came up with the company name, CoreStreet, during an impromptu session in the office. We had no product or customers yet, only the five of us, a rented office in Somerville, an ancient microwave that smelled of burnt popcorn, a dry-erase board, and some beanbag chairs. One of the engineers was a pinball machine collector and had also moved a few of his machines into the office to make it feel more "startup-y."

We were laying on those beanbags one blistery cold late-winter morning when someone started doodling on the whiteboard. They were drawing the pinball shoot—the place where the ball gets pushed through. It looked like a rocket launching.

Phil was lying back on a beanbag and offhandedly said, "Hey, ever notice how a pinball looks like a shiny little nuclear core? And what does a *core* do?" He started mumbling something about pinball shoots and streets, and generally spitballing ideas based on things he was seeing around the room.

We looked at him with a collective, "Whaaaaa?"

The wheels were already turning in his mind. Before too long, he had come up with the name CoreStreet, and a logo based on the initial doodle. While his initial version looked similar to the Atari logo, it quickly started to diverge into something not so trademarked.

The harder part was coming up with a product. As Phil and the other founders had been consultants, they were reluctant to develop anything that did not have a paying client. So, rather than begin developing a product that would be expensive and might not sell, we started spit-balling general ideas that we could test the market with, and see what people expressed interest in before building anything.

BOOTSTRAPPING

Starting a new venture is one of the most difficult financial decisions anyone can make. Before you start, you need to determine how much money you need to get to the next level of business. Then, you need to either generate enough revenue to pay bills, have enough bookable business to secure a loan, or have attracted outside investment interest.

At CoreStreet, since we did not yet have a product, we were initially started with a Friends and Family round of startup funding—mostly from Phil and the other founders—to start the business. They had given themselves a finite amount of time—through the amount of money and resources they would invest—to determine if this was a viable business. It was, therefore, our job to deliver a revenue-generating product as quickly and inexpensively as we could, or we would have to shut down.

Part of the way we accomplished that is by taking on team members who would work without pay for the first year of business. While this certainly would not work for most people, Phil's charisma allowed him to put a team together, merely by explaining his vision.

He has a way of talking that makes you believe that anything he says simply must happen—that the world would be a lesser place if we did not bring his dream into being. In a way, he is the classic visionary leader, like Steve Jobs, and employees and customers line up to follow him.

Once the team of willing volunteers was in place, we needed to in-centivize them to keep coming in and doing hard work. For the first part, Phil and I discussed what employee benefits we could provide that would not cost too much but be difficult to replicate elsewhere. What we settled on was providing no-cost PPO Health insurance for the employee and their family.

While this may seem expensive, at the time, we had under ten employees, most of them under 35, and most without children. Half were unmarried. Additionally, as a Massachusetts company, our then-Governor Mitt Romney had recently enacted a new healthcare bill that slashed health insurance rates for the state and gave incentives for employers to provide insurance to their company, as long as they contributed more than 51%. As such, the cost was minimal to us, and the benefit was substantial.

Another thing we provided was flex-time and remote work options. If we were not paying these people, we certainly did not want them to start feeling oppressed by their work schedule. A valuable lesson I had learned from game design: keep your users happily engaged, and they will keep playing. In this case, to keep people willingly working for us for free, we needed to incentivize them with the resources we had. Not everyone would have had savings, so by giving people the flexibility to work around another job, life situation, or whatever, we were able to attract and keep some fantastic talent.

In my case, while health insurance was a huge burden removed, I still needed to find a source of income. I had roughly a year of unemployment that I could pull in from my previous company—thanks to an extension that Massachusetts had ordered—but that could not support my husband and me beyond rent and utilities. If I were going to work for CoreStreet, I needed to get creative.

The first thing I did was eliminate every recurring subscription I had and lowered our cell phone and internet plans to the cheapest available. I canceled our cable bill and began scouring garage sales, online circulars, and local shops for items I could sell on eBay and Craigslist. Then I created a spreadsheet of all the local stores and their sales items and joined a coupon-clipping club, which brought my average grocery shopping bill to under $5 a week.

Now that I had met our survival-level needs, I began to try to do better. I learned about mystery shopping and joined every mystery shopping company in Massachusetts, Maine, and New Hampshire. I spent at least 20 hours a week performing mystery shops, which brought in an average of $15,000 extra for the year—not to mention all the clothing, services, and food I earned from the shops. I also took a side job as a retail item demonstrator, doing popup demonstrations of innovative technology in the department and big box stores. I became addicted to bootstrapping—and before too long, I had replaced my salary and bettered the quality of life for myself and my husband.

Within one year, CoreStreet had its funding, and I had a regular salary again—and I had learned a lot of new skills that would be useful for years to come.

CLIMBING THE LADDER

Coming up with our business case was not quite as easy as the logo—we knew we wanted to be involved in security but were not sure quite how.

We hired some smart people, though, and within a few years, we were selling radio-frequency identification (RFID) enabled door locks to government contractors and beyond. My role there morphed from Phil's Executive Assistant to HR Manager—complete with the additional training I needed for the growing company. I was completely outside of my comfort zone and even my skill set, but I was still in the tech industry, and the work was interesting enough. I was able to support my husband through school.

I thought I was content.

And then, one day, when I was filing paperwork in the HR Room, I started crying. I broke down, sobbing, and crumpled to the floor. Within a few minutes, the CFO, Jim, walked into the room and saw me there. He asked what was wrong.

"I don't know. Something's not right."

We talked for a while. I realized that not only was I drastically underpaid (more than 65% less than the next lowest employee), I was in a position that was simply not right for me. I was just working for a paycheck—and I was not even appropriately appreciated.

Something had to change.

Jim immediately issued me a raise—with back pay—and apologized for the oversight. He explained that he was new and had not gotten around to checking everyone's compensation packages yet. "If I'd known, I would have corrected that immediately."

The other things were not so easy to fix. In my mind, it should not have taken a new CFO running a comparable wage analysis to notice a discrepancy; there should have been someone who cared about me and was looking out for me.

Since I did not feel that, I started to look for another job. I quickly found one—back in game design and left Phil and CoreStreet behind.

With all the new management and people skills gleaned from working at CoreStreet, I was much better at understanding community management. I thrived at the new game studio, talking to customers and vendors alike. I also knew that this role was likely not going to be permanent—game studios are fraught with uncertainty—so I always had my eye on where I could go next.

Eventually, I moved to a position as an Account Manager for a company that manages Charitable Giving for large corporations. On the surface, it was different from anything I had ever done before—utterly different industry, a hybrid of a sales and support role—it was not something I would have applied for myself.

However, I found it intriguing. The world of non-profits interested me, and I wanted to learn more. They offered me the position at my highest salary to date, and the opportunity to change the world in a real, authentic way.

I went home to celebrate my success.

2. Uncertainty

ROUTINES

Every morning for five years, I walked through our house, down the stairs, through the hallway, and through the kitchen, where I picked up my keys, coat, and shoes to head out to the driveway and head to work.

Every single one of those mornings, Leon would hug me when I was at the back door and kiss me on the cheek before I left.

Bastian would trail behind us, watching the daily procession.

He did not miss a day.

Until one day, Leon had enough. He could not live another day in Massachusetts. He was tired of the weather, like the unseasonably cold winters. He could not stand the legal code that he believed were violating his rights. A litany of negative experiences had eaten away at him for years, and he needed to escape.

He told me that he was getting on a plane and never coming back to Boston. He was moving to California, and the choice was mine: to follow him or not. His willingness to join me in Boston had benefited *my* career, and while he had spent his time earning a degree in business, he still longed to fly. The announcement was sudden and unexpected. Honestly, it was more of an ultimatum.

In some ways, it was not surprising. Leon wanted to leave the Boston area; he was born in Hawaii, on an island where the sun is always out, the water is warm, and it is never below 60 degrees. New England winters are bitterly cold, gray, and the snowfalls are often unbearable. Nonetheless, he tried to enjoy living there. He bought a boat for the short summers and a snowmobile for the long winters. He tried to find what joy he could in the location. But after so many years, he could not handle it anymore. So, he abruptly left, and Bastian and I were all alone in the house.

The morning after I drove Leon to the airport, I prepared for work as I always did. I showered, got dressed, and walked down the stairs. Bastian was with me, at my side.

I started walking down the hallway, and as I reached the kitchen, he trotted ahead of me, which was unusual. He then hopped up onto the counter across from the door and sat there, staring at me. I put on my shoes and my coat, then grabbed my keys and bag, and reached for the door, when I heard:

"Mrowr."

I looked at him, and he had raised one paw. I leaned over, and he put his paw on my shoulder, lifted himself a little bit, and put his nose on my cheek. He then sat back down on the counter and started looking at me again.

I looked at him.

He looked at me.

I goggled.

I pet him on the head, opened the door, and went to work.

For the next few weeks, this became the new routine. Every day, Bastian gave me a hug and a kiss on my way out the door. He somehow knew Leon was not coming back, and he was telling me that we would be all right.

HELP FROM UNEXPECTED PLACES

I loved Leon, and I wanted to be with him, so there was no question in my mind—I agreed to relocate. We prepared by selling most of our household items, and I decided to quit my job. When I broke the news to my company's CEO, he surprised me by suggesting that I open a California branch of the company. I am forever grateful to him for not accepting my resignation, as it left me with at least one single point of certainty. My only plan was to keep my marriage together, and that meant more to me than a paycheck. Something about this commitment to my husband resonated with my employer: his decision and willingness to trust me helped to give me the security and resolve to get me through this time and to continue along this otherwise uncertain path.

I spent the next month downsizing our old, drafty, 3000 square foot house that had been standing in one form or another from the 1600s. I had to eliminate most of our possessions, with the remainder having to fit in my car, a small storage unit, and a 47-foot sailboat gifted to us from my parents that was to be our new home in San Diego. The problem was that I was never a water person. I get severe motion sickness in cars, and the idea of spending an extended length of time on a sailboat, let alone living on one, made me nervous. But it was what Leon wanted to do, so I did it.

For someone who has never made a cross-country move, this might not sound too difficult, but even in the best of circumstances, moving is never smooth. I was alone, and I had less than one month to try to decide what things we could not live without, what would be nice to have if we had room, and then sell, donate or throw out the rest.

I tried to hold a yard sale, but I learned how woefully unprepared I was for that when a neighbor, whom I had never met in my seven years of living there, came over to buy something. She took one look at my pathetic display and said, "Oh, girl, no. Just . . . No."

Within minutes, an army of women and children invaded my lawn and started cataloging, tagging, organizing, and hawking my items. My neighbor asked if I had anything else I to sell, and I directed her to my attic and garage.

For the next two days, she ran my yard sale like a machine. I had a fantastic time talking and laughing with them. Still, I also got a few lessons on selling—and how to accept help gracefully.

Another kind stranger I found on Craigslist saved me from accidentally donating antique tools and equipment because I had no inkling of their actual value. He helped to find me homes for things and to carry heavy items that I could not move. Once more, I discovered that my story was making a connection with people, and I was finding help everywhere I turned.

I'M ON A BOAT!

The reason Leon chose a boat instead of a more traditional form of housing was that he had a grand business idea. It was a way for us to be together but still earn a living. He wanted to create a luxury cruise line - only on small boats that were 100-150 feet. If we were going to do this, we needed to live on a boat, so we could at least understand what we were getting ourselves into. We had to immerse ourselves into this new way of life and then see where it would take us. It was an entirely distinct experience from living on land. We did not get to go for walks spontaneously or take an impulsive shopping trip. It was not the same.

A month after Leon's declaration, I arrived in San Diego. Our new home was a 47-foot Hunter Passage Center Cockpit sailboat, 15 feet longer than the one we recently sold in Boston—and three times the overall size. It was so large, Leon needed to take classes to captain it, which would also ensure that we could insure it.

I continued to work remotely for a company in Massachusetts, saving money every way I could, because I did not know how long I would stay employed. As I had been working for startups and small companies my whole career, I had learned not to trust a paycheck for long.

However, shortly after I moved to California, Leon decided that he wanted to fly again. The airlines had finally started to hire again, and in his mind, once a pilot, always a pilot. I did not agree with his decision—primarily since he would not be based in San Diego. I remembered how much he had given up for me in Boston, though, so it was my turn to support him. He left for two months to Texas for flight training, and l was alone again. Once he completed training, the job had him home about seven days a month, with the rest of the time stationed elsewhere.

I followed him across the country, only to be abandoned on a rocking boat that I never wanted. I was starting to feel loneliness, and the beginnings of depression swirling around. I felt trapped and helpless to change the situation. I was at least happy to have Bastian, his cat, to keep me company.

I threw myself into my work—going from morning to night, rarely changing out of my pajamas or leaving the boat. I did not even stop to visit my parents, who were a mere ten miles away.

PHIL'S RETURN

About this time, Phil Libin had an idea for a new company called "Ribbon" and contacted me. I told him that I had a job, and I could not see myself leaving a *good-paying* one for something that was not going to pay anything. I had already given him five years in Boston, where I had ultimately felt unappreciated and burned out. I did not think it was wise to do it again, especially with Leon not earning much money. Phil acquiesced.

When Leon returned to flying, he quickly remembered that the idealized illusion of the job bore little resemblance to the reality of it. The hours were distressing and unpredictable; the pay was poor; the mechanics did not treat the aircraft very well; the passengers were horrific. Honestly, being a commercial pilot was horrible. The only thing he liked about it was being in the sky, so eventually, he quit again. His resignation letter was: "I miss my wife; I'm going home." He told me the chief pilot was skeptical, and they tried to give him his next assignment as he was walking out the door.

While Leon no longer had a job and a set routine, I still did. My job consisted of me managing accounts where I was the single point of contact for clients located on the East and West coasts. A typical workday started around 5 A.M. and ended sometime after 6 P.M. to ensure proper coverage. The routines I started while Leon was flying remained firmly in place even after he returned. I was now a top performer at work and felt that my work ethic was the reason.

Even so, I looked forward to any break that I could get in my daily schedule of "Wake Up. Open Laptop. Work all day. Close Laptop. Sleep." About six months later, an opportunity to present at a conference in San Francisco appeared, so I flew up there for the day. Phil Libin again contacted me and asked if he could meet with me. I told him that I was going to be busy, but he was welcome to attend, and we could meet after it was over. He showed up before the conference started, helped me to set up my booth, and then waited with me all day until the conference ended, even helping me to make my presentation.

During our meal together, Phil began his next attempt to recruit me. He explained that the company was no longer called Ribbon. It was called Evernote and would merge with another company with a similar idea. He emphasized that he wanted me to join because he needed me.

I pressed him for details and some sort of job description. He responded by telling me he did not yet know what I would be doing, but he wanted me to join his team, and we would figure things out as we went along. I did not want to take this job merely because Phil Libin wanted me there. I had a job that was paying me well, and with Leon not flying again, I was concerned about how this latest offer would affect our relationship. This company was in San Francisco, and it was a startup, and startups do not have the best track records of making payroll. I declined.

Leon was struggling. He started selling motorcycles to stay busy, but mentally he was drifting. He needed a job that would get him home at night because his priority was his marriage, and he wanted to be on the boat and be able to go out, sail, and do things together. After months of floundering, he threw himself back into working on our business plan.

At the beginning of 2008, we started to travel to other countries, trying to work with governments around the world to reach favorable agreements where we could launch our business model. Leon had received his Master's license, which meant he could operate the size vessels we wanted. He was now not only certified as a captain of a plane but was also now a real boat captain. We decided that the next logical step was to go on an immersion trip. Because we were not going to run our business in the United States, we wanted to spend time living on a boat outside the country to see how that would go.

It took a few months to get everything prepared for this latest adventure. As part of the preparation, we took a ten-day trip to marina towns within the Sea of Cortez, Mexico, to find our future home. We finished the trip feeling renewed in the certainty that we were doing the right thing, having located the perfect place to live.

Unfortunately, when we returned to San Diego, something was amiss. Bastian, the cat, Leon's loyal friend and companion for many years, had disappeared. Leon was devastated. For weeks, he would walk among the docks, calling the cat's name. He put up flyers everywhere, and still, we could not find Bastian.

While no animal could replace another, Leon gradually came to accept that Bastian was gone, and he missed that companionship. Around eight weeks after Bastian's disappearance, we adopted Morgan, a Bengal kitten. He was not going to be old enough for us to take him home for another six weeks, but we visited him as often as we wished. Leon begrudgingly started to pack up Bastian's toys.

Not long after, there was a knock on our boat. Leon popped his head above deck; it was the caretaker for the marina. He was holding one of Bastian's flyers and told us that he thought he found our cat.

For the first time in weeks, there was color in Leon's face. He ran up the stairs and nearly accosted the man, yet he could only choke out the words, "Show me." Sure enough, within an hour, Bastian had returned to us, completing our family once more. Leon was finally happy again.

Now that our preparations were complete and we were ready to depart, Phil Libin came back to me a third time. This time, as was his way, he popped up a chat window with a quick "Yo." After I responded, his message began in earnest:

"All right, we've got things in order. We can pay for your salary. We're able to do this. We're a real company now, and I know what I want you to do. I want you to take over support for Evernote. It's not much now, but I see the company as customer-oriented, it's all about the users. And this company is going to grow—it's going to be huge. And the only way it's going to grow properly is if we take care of these users and make sure that their needs are taken care of from the beginning on."

That sounded like everything I wanted to hear. It was perfect for me, but I was about to leave the country, so I would not be able to come to an office. I was certainly not leaving my husband for a job again. I told Libin that if there were a job for Leon, I might consider his proposal.

In his quick, matter of fact way, Phil wrote the words that would radically alter the course of my life. He responded, "Well, both of those can be accommodated. Let's work that out."

In September 2008, both Leon and I started with Evernote. I was full-time in my position, and Leon was a contractor. I was one of the first full-time employees with Evernote after it merged with the original team. The idea of hiring Leon and I was to build a support infrastructure from the ground up. We were to become intricately involved with Engineering, Quality Assurance, Business Development, and Marketing, and, of course, Customer Service, which was critical from the very beginning. We were involved in everything from the start, and even remotely, we had access to whatever we needed. Phil Libin was and is impressive in that he saw the value of excellent customer service right from the onset.

Good customer service was revolutionary at the time—and continues to be. Back in 2008, very few tech companies cared about Customer Service in this way. Zappos was one of the few online companies that had a reputation for their service, and there were no startup teams as small as we were that spent the effort we made on their customers. In fact, at the time, many new companies were turning to "No Support" models, where there are often no contact forms or any other means of asking for assistance. Small companies expected the customer to search Google for help rather than contacting them directly. They used "choose your own adventure" self-help forms that published knowledge-based articles, bringing the user into a loop that never gave access to a human being.

Libin was adamant that everyone would receive help, in a reasonable amount of time, whether or not they had paid us any money. "Everyone is our customer," he would say.

We got all the groundwork in place and waited a couple of more months to make sure that everything was solid with the company, and then Leon and I set off for Mexico. It was an excellent place to begin our trip because it was not so far from the States, and we could get back quickly if necessary. As this entire undertaking was wrought with uncertainty, we wanted to ensure again that we had at least a foundation from which to work. We decided to move the boat to Ensenada (which is only an hour's drive south of San Diego) for a month before going further south into Mexico.

ENSENADA

In December of 2008, Leon sailed without me to Ensenada, Mexico, where we would help build our little piece of the now multi-billion-dollar company. Initially, there were only a few thousand users and only a handful of employees, and we had a vital role to play. It was quite an adventure for us to be sailing around Mexico on our boat, creating a new department entrusted with the company's most valuable asset—its customers—and helping develop Evernote.

Everything was going well—we had reliable internet, great food, we liked the people on our marina, and we docked next to one of the Black Pearl filming boats from the movie Pirates of the Caribbean.

On December 31, Leon and I had our first taste of culture shock. In Ensenada, people grow up speaking English alongside Spanish. They are close enough to the United States that they can receive some English-speaking television channels. So, when we were invited to a New Year's Eve party at the marina's hotel, we naively thought it would be the same as any other party we had been to before.

For the most part, it was, but there were some subtle differences. Instead of the customary champagne, there was tequila in abundance. Waiters were selling bottles of a popular grapefruit soda to mix with the tequila to make a drink not-unlike a fizzy margarita. We had never seen this before, but our tablemates assured us it was quite popular.

What confused me, however, were the grapes laid out on the table. I thought they were there to eat as an appetizer and picked one up to eat when my hand was smacked hard by the little girl to the left of me.

"Don't eat that! It's for the wishes!"

I looked at her, incredulous. I was so shocked that I could not entirely construe what she was saying. Her father stepped in to help me out. "There is a tradition in Mexico that we should have a wish for each month of the new year. We lock in our wish by eating grapes—twelve grapes—each for the first twelve seconds of the new year. In that way, we will make our luck real, and bring it into ourselves."

Our first night's foibles notwithstanding, that month in Ensenada was exciting. I was staying in San Diego during the week and visiting on weekends because after Bastian's adventures, we now had a kitten who was too young to be brought into Mexico. I would have to wait with him in San Diego until the spring of 2009 before I could fully join Leon.

For his part, Leon spent his weeks working from the boat, hanging around the marina, and otherwise waiting for me to arrive; he did not venture out and explore the city. When I was there, and we went out together, he was often confused by the streets that suddenly ended, turned into dirt roads, road signs that made no sense, and the lack of parking spaces that were large enough for our truck.

Once the month in Ensenada was finished, and Leon was sure he could live in Mexico, it was time to move the boat to its next port of call, Cabo San Lucas. The trip from Ensenada to Cabo takes approximately four days and should not be done alone. As I was a full-time employee, there was no way I could take four days off to make the trip. Leon was only working part-time, so he could make up his hours at the end of the week.

He called his sister and found another experienced sailor to help and set sail. They were lucky—while that area is notoriously windy, they had lovely weather on the way down and a great trip. Unfortunately, he was now about 1200 miles away from me, not close enough to visit on the weekend.

While our older cat, Bastian, could immediately enter Mexico and leave with Leon, I had to wait three more months for the kitten, Morgan, to be old enough to enter into Mexico. As soon as he turned six months old, we had all the proper paperwork, and everything was good to go.

The boat was now docked in San Jose del Cabo, roughly twenty minutes north of Cabo San Lucas, Mexico. Like Ensenada, we decided this would be an excellent place to stay for a month or so while we got our bearings. Our rationale was that this was a tourist area—almost everyone speaks English, the food is familiar, and we could buy supplies readily if we needed anything.

When it was finally time for me to join him, Leon flew up to San Diego. As he had sailed down, I had our truck and the rest of our possessions with me. We packed the truck with only the things we thought we would need (clothes, some food, and boat supplies). A boat does not have much room, and we had already packed it pretty full. We also decided to bring our jet ski and motorcycle as well. We figured those would be useful things to have as we could have additional forms of transportation on land and water if we needed them.

CUSTOMS

It was five o'clock on Friday afternoon when we decided to get on the road and get across the border. Unfortunately, we could not have picked a worse time to start, because five o'clock rush hour in San Diego is crazy. Leon hated traffic—"hate" is not a strong enough word to describe his feelings about traffic and congestion. So, our trip did not begin on a positive note.

Leon figured that by leaving at five o'clock, we would drive for about six or seven hours, then we would stop around midnight, sleep, and then drive the rest of the way the next day. That way, we would have all of Sunday to unpack and get acclimated. Unfortunately, it did not work that way. We started in San Diego only about thirty miles from the border of Mexico, yet it took us an hour and a half to get to the border.

The problems did not stop there. Because we had the Jet Ski, we had to "import" it coming into the country as a marine vessel. We could not directly drive across the border as most people do; this took us two hours on a Friday night because the customs agents were confused as to how to process a boat coming across on land. They were trying to tell us that we had to go to Ensenada, via water, with the Jet Ski, or cross at another border because they did not know how to classify it.

After being in traffic for an hour and a half and then attempting to maintain a modicum of politeness with the Mexican officials for two hours, Leon started to get slightly agitated. Meanwhile, Morgan was in the truck, and this six-month-old kitten started meowing like crazy. We still had not gotten anything taken care of by the customs officers, so my bright idea was that maybe I could use the cat. I took him out of the truck and started walking him around on the floor of the Immigration office.

Suddenly, everybody wanted to take his picture, touch, and pet him. They were curious as to what he was. I told them that he was a Leopardito because he is a Bengal, and he does look like a little leopard. At six months old, he looked like a full-grown cat. Even then, his paws and his head were more prominent than a typical house cat. This kitten suddenly became a spectacle in the office, so much so that we caused all work to stop.

Our ingenuity in using Morgan is how we ended up getting through customs. Our cat managed to get it done. Suddenly the appropriate paperwork appeared; they had magically figured out how to import the Jet Ski. We did not know our little feline friend could be such a source of influence. Our decision to get another cat had far-reaching and unforeseen results. Sometimes we do not know how much even the smallest decisions we make today can positively influence our lives.

By the time we crossed the border, it was nine o'clock at night. We still had not eaten and had only traveled 45 miles. Even the kitten was cranky; it was then that we realized that we were about to embark on a thousand-mile journey, and we had not brought any cat food. We drove to Ensenada, Mexico, pulled into the familiar marina hotel, and hoped for room service. They did have it, but nothing was suitable on the menu for the kitten; there was no tuna or anything else that we could chop up for a meal.

Desperate pet parents that we were, we ordered garlic butter shrimp and then chopped it up into small pieces. We gave him a plate of the shrimp, smothered in butter so that he would want to eat it. It was funny, in a way, because the whole reason I had stayed behind was to take care of his needs. Still, somehow, we managed to go on a trip without bringing anything for the cat. This experience indeed stayed with Morgan, since he adores anything with garlic, even chewing on cloves directly sometimes.

The next day we got on the road and drove about thirteen hours to San Ignacio, which was halfway through the Baja Peninsula. We were going to a beautiful resort that I had heard of, a farm in the middle of Mexico, where they cultivate date trees and raise livestock. They had yurts set up as individual hotel rooms, each with a separate theme, and each more beautiful than the last. They gave us a room that had a hot tub, and we could bring in our cat without any trouble.

Our yurt was beautiful. It had a separate bathroom, a Jacuzzi outside, and was in the most beautiful oasis. I felt like I was in Costa Rica, Barbados, or some other resort location. It was gorgeous. We let the cat out, and he ran around sniffing everything. We were preparing to feed him the cat food we had gotten from a truck stop on the road, but the staff insisted on bringing Morgan some fresh food. He has always been treated like a little prince in hotels, and this was no different.

Once we settled in the room, we went to the hotel's communal dinner table. Typically, this kind of thing is an issue for me, as I do not eat red meat or pork, but they had so many side dishes, it was perfect. They fed me a cake made with dates that I have tried to replicate but have never succeeded. I still have never been able to find dates that tasted so sweet and as good as at theirs. Every time we made that trip back and forth to San Diego, I always wanted to stay there, but it never worked out again.

The next morning was Sunday. We had gotten a good night's rest, and due to a gross miscalculation, we only had about seven hours left of the drive to go. It was an uneventful ride the rest of the way down to Los Cabos, and when we got there, we unloaded the truck. Fortunately, Morgan was super excited about everything. He figured out his favorite place to hang out on the boat, and he stayed there for the next three years.

CABO SAN LUCAS

We made it to San Jose del Cabo to our new international life on a boat. I was amazed at the things I noticed living on the water away from an enclosed marina. The waves' crashing sound was refreshing and calming while the motion of the boat was, at times, a bit rocky. The isolation of living on a boat also brought regular activity to life. We now had the two cats together on the boat. Morgan was now a part of our family, joining Bastian, our beautiful white cat we had had for seven years.

While Morgan adjusted readily to his new life, Bastian did not. He hated having a "little brother." He had been an "only cat" for his whole life and was not pleased to have so many changes. He was with Leon when we were living apart, he was living with us in Boston, and now he had to change his life dramatically and live an aquatic life with an unwanted sibling. Morgan loved everything about the boat: Bastian hated it. He hated the kitten and grew nervous at every motion and noise. The time he was gone for eight full weeks changed him. When he returned, he was not the same cat. He had been sweet and caring, the kind of cat that would cuddle with me when I was alone. When he came back, he would not let anyone touch him, and having a kitten around exacerbated things.

That is how it is in life—transitions and uncertainty. Making the shift from Boston to a boat was a meaningful change. Nevertheless, what is life without risk? Like Bastian, too many people run away from change and are suspicious of transition. Eventually, we all face things that are different or challenging. We often make the mistake of choosing to run away from responsibility, commitment, transition, opposition, and opportunity. Change is not easy, especially when someone or something is in the way.

The first week that we were down there, we buried ourselves in our work. No sightseeing, no shopping. We did not go out anywhere and explore. After all, we were helping to build this startup business. By now, Leon was full-time, and the work started to explode. In the beginning, it started with 50,000 users, but when we came on, it had jumped to over 100,000 users.

Leon, CTO Dave Engberg, and I were the only three people doing any customer support for Evernote at the time. Engberg spent three hours a day answering forum questions on the discussion boards. That time-consuming task was most of his contribution to the Support Department (as he was busy being a CTO), which he would do on his drive home and the train. He always said that was his way to relax.

It was challenging work, and since we were finding our way, we often had to improvise. Whenever we faced something unknown or even something truly unique, we needed to be able to be self-sufficient.

There is no tangible way to control who uses software, so suddenly, we received questions from all over the world—Australia, China, Japan, across Europe—far beyond the United States. To handle the load, we had to split shifts. Leon is naturally a morning person, so he started early. I started later, and together we would cover the day. I was staying up late, and he was going to bed early. Because of this schedule, we started not to see each other very much, even though we were on this small boat.

So, there we were in Mexico, busy all day with work, with one cat keeping us up all night with his howling. Because the boat was confined, we had nowhere to put him to give us some rest. We worried about the quality of our work because we were not sleeping.

After two weeks of being there, my whole family came down for our then annual family gathering. My sister, my brother, cousins, parents, grandparents, in-laws, and all their assorted spouses, children, and partners were all with us in Cabo. We went to the hotel during the day to hang out with the family and kept going back and forth to the boat. We could not take time off from work, and it made it difficult to enjoy the family. At the time, I am not sure they understood what we were doing. This seemingly never-ending work schedule began a pattern early on with Evernote; no matter where we were for the next five and a half years, we did not take any real vacations. Even if we were on vacation, we were working.

We worked our regular hours, and while it distressed some of the family, to Leon and me, it was a lucky thing that we were able to do. We were able to go to many places and do many things. We could go to Disney World—and watch the fireworks while working from our hotel. We could visit our family—and work while they were having conversations around us. We could travel to Paris or even cruise on our boat, and the only price for being a digital nomad was that we had to work hard wherever we were—a tradeoff that we were willing to make.

My parents left us alone because they knew that we were busy, and they knew that we were working, and it was their way of not bothering us. They were polite by leaving us alone. However, to have the lifestyle we wanted, to be with each other, we had to make sacrifices. One of those sacrifices was the inability to take off in the middle of the day to go fishing for eight hours or even to socialize. Working on a boat is like telecommuting from home—the work must get done.

We did set aside time to take the family out on the sailboat. Bastian and Morgan were both on the sailboat with us, and my cousin Joe, his wife Maggie, and their daughter Mia enjoyed playing with the kitten. Maggie immediately noticed how scared, upset, and sad Bastian was. She was taken by him immediately and wanted to "save" him. Maggie and my sister hatched a plan to rescue Bastian from the "horrible" life on a sailboat. For the rest of the week of this family vacation, they went about trying to convince Leon to let them take Bastian. The thought of allowing Bastian to leave was a complicated thing for him because Bastian was his best friend, next to me, of course. He had Bastian for seven years and loved him as a member of the family. He was hoping that he would eventually become adjusted to living on the water. But what it came down to was that Bastian was a land cat, not a water cat.

By the end of the week, we were driving all around Cabo San Lucas, trying to find a veterinarian for the paperwork and shots that Bastian would need to get on an airplane. Bastian flew home with my cousin, and we only ever saw him once more after that. Unfortunately, about four years later, Bastian disappeared, and they never saw him again. Still, he had been happy, loved, and catered to there, and he was on land. He probably went off into the woods and died happily.

LA PAZ

On the weekend, everyone returned to their respective homes in the States, and we finally sailed to La Paz, Mexico, where we had always been planning to move. We were excited about the trip to La Paz. We had scouted out the area, and when we first found it, we felt like we were home. We moved the boat, but our truck was still down in San Jose del Cabo, so we had some logistics to work out because we would eventually have to drive our motorcycle back down to pick up the truck.

La Paz was a town so welcoming, lovely, and quiet that we knew we had made the right decision by choosing this peaceful town. The trip from San Jose Del Cabo to La Paz took us 18 hours. I had known it was a long sail, but it was worth it. When we pulled the boat into our slip at the marina, no fewer than eight people were waiting to help us maneuver the boat in. Some of them worked for the marina, but a lot of them were residents of the marina. They were all so friendly.

One man introduced himself as Mike, and he indicated that he lived on the next dock. He suggested we get situated and then come meet him for "sundowners," that way, we could have a drink and get to know each other. His parting words at the first meeting were an honest offer to help if we needed anything.

We had only been living on a boat for a little while before moving into Mexico, so we did not know what was "normal." We did not know anyone at all in our marina in San Jose Del Cabo; we were not there long enough to do that. On the other hand, in San Diego, we had a couple of friends we had met on our dock. The friends in San Diego had become lifelong friends, and meeting Mike that first day cemented our feeling of "coming home." Our life was once again less uncertain.

The following weekend was Easter. In Mexico, Easter is a huge holiday. Everything shuts down for a week. There is nothing open, so we thought this would be an excellent opportunity to take the drive to get the truck. We decided to go on Easter Saturday, the day after Good Friday.

We left that morning on our motorcycle around 7 A.M. Immediately, we noticed that there seemed to be a lot more people out than usual at 7 A.M. on a Saturday (although granted, we did not have much to compare this to). We could not believe how many people were active. It was only later that we discovered that Easter was a time for multiple festivities, and many people took several days, if not weeks, off from work to celebrate.

And when I say "celebrate," I am not talking about religious activities. These people were partying in the streets. Cars and trucks were swerving everywhere, and people threw beer cans out of windows. This was 7 A.M., and the people were drinking heavily and driving without a care in the world.

One thing that we kept failing to get used to was the condition of the roads and the driving habits of the locals. The two-lane highway was, in many places, filled with twists and turns, and rife with potholes. Cars were being driven erratically and passing us going extremely fast, nearly knocking our motorcycle off the road multiple times. By the time we arrived at the halfway point, in Todos Santos, we were terrified. We stopped at a convenience store and decided to rest there for a bit to get our bearings.

At that exact moment, police officers arrived. With our typical American attitude, we thought that the police would surely tell the intoxicated drivers to get off the road.

Oh, were we wrong!

Instead, without breaking stride, one officer got out of his car, walked into the convenience store, purchased a six-pack of beer, walked outside, and, without removing it from the plastic rings, opened a can of beer and began to drink it. This was something I had never seen anyone do before outside of a fraternity. With no effort, he pulled the entire six-pack up to his mouth and guzzled it down like water. Then, he got back into his car and drove off—still drinking his beer. Talk about culture shock!

Leon and I looked at each other in total amazement. We still had another 45 miles to go before we reached our destination, and by now, it was 9 a.m. More and more people were pouring out onto the streets and blocking the road, and more and more people were drunk. We did not know what to do. We were halfway there already. There were no cabs and no rental cars. Getting back on the road surrounded by drunk drivers felt like certain death. We were flabbergasted, petrified, and wondered if we would ever make it out of there. We had no choice, so we pushed on and held on for dear life.

Unbelievably, it took us almost five hours, and we were scared the entire way. We were in a foreign country, we did not fully understand the language, and Leon was full of uncertainty as to what these people were capable of doing to a few Americans who looked like lost tourists. We could have been injured, attacked, or been in an accident, and nobody would have known about it or would have been able to find us. This ride was one time I was holding on tightly to Leon—not out of love, but out of fear.

We had to continue our journey. We had started something, so we had to finish it. We got ourselves to Mexico. We were there, 1100 miles from anyone who could help us, so we had to deal with it on our own. We had gotten ourselves into this mess, and we had to get out of it, and we did.

We jumped back on the motorcycle. Staying in the right-hand lane, we avoided the drunk drivers, and we powered through.

I think it was at that point we realized that everything was going to be okay. No matter how strange the circumstances, no matter how much we did not understand, no matter what the situation, we could handle anything because we were together. In a world of uncertainty, it is essential to have someone by your side.

EVERNOTE SUPPORT

By this time, Leon became a full-time employee because Evernote had secured more funding after almost shutting down entirely a few months earlier due to financing issues related to the collapse of the stock market in 2008. That had been exceedingly difficult for Phil Libin. Still, at the last minute, a foreign investor and a fan of the company stepped in with financing. Phil's certainty that the customer was essential to success was validated, and consequently, we now had money. We could live. We could survive. And, we were on the way to becoming a viable company. Life was good. Leon and I were in Mexico; we made it over our first hurdle.

We had convinced Libin and Engberg to let us work from there, so what exactly were we doing? Much of our work at that time was answering support tickets, which were coming in from the customers. We looked at all the support tickets, and we noticed they all fell into one of two categories: routine questions that could be quickly answered because we had already answered those questions and created a "macro" to send out as a response, or they required some investigation and testing before we answered them.

At that time, there were roughly 100,000 users, and at any given time, there were 300 to 500 tickets in the queue. Almost overnight, we successfully developed both a Customer Service and Technical Support department, where Customer Service was the first line of support. This department became the base of the support infrastructure that we used for the company as it scaled worldwide.

Even though we were on this trip to spend more time with each other, we ended up spending less time with each other. Our typical workday was like this: Leon would wake up in the morning around 4, and work for about 10 hours. I would wake up around 11, and work for 10 hours. He went to sleep sometime around 7 or 8, trying not to bother me, and I tried not to disturb him when I went to sleep at midnight.

It seems weird, but we got to see more "inside" of each other. Leon and I were not spending much time actively together, but we focused on our combined task. In the morning, when he woke up, he would see a message from me saying something like, "I wrote you this program to save you some time," or, "I wrote you this macro that will automate this answer for you." We would do things for each other that showed each other how much we cared.

We worked on weekends unofficially because there was no way that the two of us could keep up otherwise. If I had 50 new tickets added into my queue each day, I could complete 50 to 80, and Leon would answer around 120, but we still got new tickets—about 300 to 500 each day. In addition, people would respond to the tickets that we had out, adding to that number. Engberg helped us by answering questions on our forums as well as anything we needed to "escalate" to him. At one point, he was up to about 5,000 answers on our discussion boards. Engberg was a legend, and that became something that our users loved.

By the time we got to a million users, it had become apparent there was no way we could do this job by ourselves anymore. We started to look around for help, but it was not an easy task. We interviewed staff all around the globe, but we could not find anyone who met our require-ments because we were very, very selective.

I did not want somebody who would only follow a script because there simply was not one, and honestly, I did not have time to write one. We needed people who could think for themselves and make decisions based on the questions presented. We also needed to find a team within our price range. We managed to hire an outsourced team in India that was not only affordable for our startup company but also met our other requirements.

We needed to have a team that we could train to find the answers. The group in India was intrigued by the challenge, so the team expanded to include them. We later learned that they did not put traditional Customer Service agents on our unit. Instead, they gave us QA people. They heard our requirements and understood that what we wanted were testers, so they gave us QA people, and they let them test every single ticket that came in. Those guys were smart, but most importantly, they were fast.

We hired one person initially, and then Evernote started growing so fast that within six months, we hired another person. It turned out that what they did was hire a Leon, and then they hired a Heather. What I mean by that is they hired a Customer Service guy first to tee things up, and then they hired a Technical Support guy to do the testing for the more difficult questions.

When I saw that happening, I realized that was the perfect solution; from then on, I always wanted to hire in pairs. I always wanted to hire a Customer Service person and a Tech Support person and pair them up. My rationale was, if they trained and worked together, they would understand each other and trust each other's work the way that Leon and I did. They learned how each other worked; they knew what the other one could handle and how their partner would answer the questions and what their strengths and weaknesses were.

I felt I was onto something. Not only did these people work well together, but also they did not always work the same hours. They were able to select cases that the other one would excel at and tee things up for each other. When I started to hire in-house, I decided I would try to recruit in teams like this as well and see how it worked.

With my first experiment at Evernote, I had the Customer Service person work in the morning, and the Tech Support person work at night. It worked well. They trusted each other, and they could do it. I think that this kind of pairing is vital for every company. If people know each other's strengths and weaknesses and can rely on them, a symbiotic system that benefit employees and the company as a whole. It was perfect, and it showed us that we could trust what we already had.

This system did not evolve through trial and error—this was something that happened organically, which produced something exceptional. That was the beginning of working in La Paz.

Our entire adventure was fraught with uncertainty from the moment we started. Still, we learned a valuable lesson: not having a rigid predetermined plan is no reason to avoid taking risks. The future is always unpredictable, but inaction can often lead to frustration, dissatisfaction, and stagnation. Uncertainty should motivate us and may lead to an exciting and fruitful journey through life.

Are you faced today with the uncertainty of the choices you know you need to make? I can only encourage you to have the confidence to take that first step and expect the best. It is the only way you will find out where any particular road or course of action will lead.

NAVIGATING AN UNCERTAIN LIFE

Everyone has a desire for change. Whether it is flipping through TV channels, clicking from one article to another on a website, or setting off on an adventure to another country, our need for variety is invigorating.

It is remarkably simple: no one likes to be bored. While the stability brought to you by certainty can give strength, too much confidence can lead to stagnancy.

To attain and maintain a healthy and balanced life, you will need to juggle the need for Certainty and Uncertainty. Finding that balance is something only you can do, but here are some examples of ways to fill your need for Uncertainty:

LEARN – The world is continuously changing, and there are always articles to read, the latest movies and DVDs to watch, innovative podcasts to listen to, and new people to meet.

PLAY – Artists give us new ways to view the world with their different formats of expression. We can immerse ourselves in a novel, watch along during a movie, feel and experience music, and navigate the emotional twists and turns throughout. It is a playground that is always ready for us to use.

EXPLORE – Changing your location by going somewhere "different" that is outside your daily routine or taking a vacation is a wonderful way to fill this need. You can start by simply trying something new on a restaurant menu.

DO – Starting a hobby, or joining a club, is a fantastic way to increase the variety of activities you have in your life. By introducing this healthy change into your life, it will positively offset your need for Certainty.

INNOVATE – Creating something new is the ultimate way of introducing change. Innovation can take many forms: you can sew a dress without a pattern, build something with Lego blocks, create a recipe or generate something for your business—the possibilities are as limitless as your mind. By innovating, you will always be able to fill this need.

3.
Significance

LANGUAGE BARRIERS

Significance is the quality of being unique, of being worthy, of doing something that "matters." It is the desire to feel unique and different. It is one of my least essential needs and one of Leon's greatest.

Everyone wants attention no matter what the need for or the extent of that recognition might be. People want credit for the work they do, the things they can do, the status they have, or even the things they own. This desire for recognition or status is something that can cause conflict and drive people apart; the result of this wedge can be abject loneliness.

As I consider this particular human need, my mind drifts back to life on the Mexican roads. They were speed limits, but no one seemed to pay any attention to them. Instead of having police officers give tickets for exceeding the speed limit, there were speed bumps with a yellow sign that had the word TOPE written on it, which provided the warning. Newly arrived, we had no idea what that sign meant. The word means "stop," but the *stop* signs in Mexico say "Alto." A diagonal yellow warning sign was right there in the street—if only we knew what type of warning it was.

We were in the truck driving about 50 miles an hour when suddenly, we hit what amounted to a 1½ foot high solid barrier in the middle of the road. We did not see it because it was not painted or marked in any way, and it was dark. I was sure we had broken an axle.

This speed bump was anything but subtle. It was as if there were a wall between us and the rest of the road. Leon was driving at the time, and he pulled over because he thought we had hit and killed something.

To our relief, it turned out that everything was fine: we had only hit the speed bump so fast that it had made a lot of noise. We were cautious after that episode, and as soon as we got back on the road, we saw that there was another "Tope" sign indicating one-half mile away. As we approached, Leon slowed down to about 5 miles an hour.

Our truck was a Ford F-350, roughly 20 feet long, with both an extended bed and an oversized cabin. Despite, or perhaps because of the size of the vehicle, even though we drove very slowly, we still felt every inch of that bump. I often wondered what it would feel like for a Mexican low rider car to go over them.

After this first encounter with the *TOPE* sign, we became alert whenever we saw a sign. The next day we saw the sign and then scrutinized the road looking for the impediment, but we did not see it. Suddenly we hit something, and we were bewildered since we had been looking for a speed bump. It turned out to be a speed dip, a big hole, like a sinkhole in the road. It was only on one side of the way—our side—and the *TOPE* sign was there. We now contextually surmised that *TOPE* did not merely mean speed bump, but figured it meant "road hazard" or "slow" or maybe even literally "stop" (though that wouldn't make much sense to have two different stop signs). We accepted 'slow down significantly' as the interpretation of *TOPE* for the rest of our time in Mexico.

I realize that in our quest for significance, there are times we will encounter speed bumps and speed dips that force us to slow down significantly. Arriving at a destination is always not dependent on maintaining the same speed. So, on many occasions, though we were still on the move and driving at a moderate rate, we slowed down a bit, and in doing so, we saw things we might have missed.

GRACEFUL EXITS

Every four or five months, we would take a long weekend trip to San Diego. After a week in La Paz, we would drive up to San Diego to my parents' house to buy boat supplies and other American goodies and then come back. Some things, like sailcloth and anchor chains, we could only get in the States because they would be too expensive to ship. Since people from the surrounding marines often drove to San Diego, it was not uncommon to ask those making the trip to bring back the desired items. When we were not making the trip, we would ask others for something (I am *particularly* fond of Entenmann's coffeecake), and when it was our turn, we would bring things back for our community of ex-pats.

We usually offered to take up to two passengers, as well—if someone needed to cross the border. While most people declined, on one occasion, our offer was accepted by a man from another marina named Archie. He and Morgan were to be fast friends in the back seat for the next 1,100 miles.

Archie, and his wife Starr, lived in a different marina outside of La Paz, on a boat remarkably similar to ours—with one significant difference: their boat was not in the water. In a recent hurricane, they had taken on some minor damage, and while the boat was still livable, it needed repairs before it was safe to float again. He needed to go to San Diego to pick up supplies to fix the boat—but he was not in a hurry back.

"Where are you going next?" I asked him.

"Starr and I are going to retire to Oregon. We have a plot of land that is 35 acres, overlooking a beautiful stream. It has got the most amazing trees that reach as high as the sun. We have been building a house there for the last 25 years—stone by stone. Every time we go somewhere new, we collect more stones and then bring them up there, then I set the stone into the mortar. There is something so satisfying about building your own house. When it is complete, that's when we'll move in."

Leon let out a little chuckle from the driver's seat. "How can you be sure you will ever finish? Won't you just keep saying, 'Hey, let's add on another room? I feel a trip to Antigua coming on.'"

Archie disagreed and said, "Of course, we'll always have a little wanderlust. But you have to admit when you are done. You have to be able to say, 'This thing is finished' and move on to the next phase, or you'll be stuck in a rut all your life."

Leon and I looked at each other, nodded, and kept driving. It was a heavy conversation at the time and made an impression.

PAVMIENTO

We had decided to set off incredibly early in the morning—while it was still dark out—as all of us were early risers, and we had a long way to go.

All of us had made this trip before, but we brought maps and a GPS navigation system to be safe. As planned, we started at five in the morning, but for some reason, we were all overly tired that day. Before too long, Archie and I nodded off, leaving Leon to both drive and navigate. Predictably, Leon made a wrong turn, or instead, he was supposed to turn right but went straight instead.

When Archie and I finally woke up, nothing looked familiar. When I questioned Leon about where we were, he stated that he was, in fact, following the map, and we were on Route 1. He maintained that there was only one highway in Mexico, and it went all the way up the Baja Peninsula. The sun had not yet risen, and we could not see very well, but we did eventually see signs that read, "Route 1A." Route 1A was the older version of Route 1; unfortunately, no one paved the older version of Route 1.

Luckily, Ford designed F-350 trucks to go off-road, so we were not worried until the pavement became cracked. I asked Leon to turn around, so we could figure out where we were, but he kept insisting that we were on the right road. As we drove on a cracked road that was supposed to be a major highway, Leon still convinced himself that he was on the right path.

A man and his ego!

I decided it was no use arguing and considered going back to sleep and letting him figure it out on his own.

Leon finally pulled up in front of a convenience store and suggested that since Archie and I spoke Spanish, we should find out if we were on the right road.

Archie and I got out of the car, went into the store, and asked how far it would be to Loreto, which was the next major town on the road we were on. The storekeeper said to us that it was 25 Kilometers "that way" and pointed us forward along the same route.

I looked at Archie, because the road did not look all that great, and I wanted to turn back. His Spanish was better than mine, so he decided to come at this a different way. He asked if there any paved highway on the road to Loreto, and the shopkeeper nodded vehemently, said 25 Kilometers, and then said, "Pavmiento!"

Archie and I looked at each other, shrugged, and figured that this horrible road was an alternate route, and we would reach pavement again soon.

We got back on the road with a truck and a car now in front of us, and vehicles coming alongside us because it was a two-way road with highway markers for Highway 1A on it. At this point, Leon decided that he was ready to turn around. We protested and told him to keep going, and the majority ruled, so he remained on that road.

The cars all turned off together onto a side road, leaving only us and the truck, which made a turn and went right up the cliff face. Leon simply put the Ford into four-wheel drive, said a quick prayer, and followed it up the mountain. By this time, we were used to not knowing where we were going, so it did not seem so out of place.

We followed that truck and were soon going from boulder to boulder; I kept saying aloud, "This can't possibly be a road."

Every time, no sooner had I said those words did we see a highway marker on the road, followed by another, and another marking the way. Soon, on the other side of the cliff face, we were stunned to see a car, not a truck, descending.

We continued this way for over an hour, boulder to boulder, up and around the mountain until finally, we were back on something that looked paved but was more of a packed-down dirt road. We breathed a mild sigh of relief, until to our dismay, the truck turned off the road.

My heart sank because we still did not see anything familiar, and our guide vehicle would no longer be there for us. Everywhere we looked, there were only rocks and mountains, and some long-forgotten skeletons. We were in the middle of a valley, and it looked like the land of the lost; I was ready to cry.

Leon stopped the truck, and Archie went outside to talk with the driver of the one we had been following. After a few minutes, he returned with the information that we should keep going straight through the center of the valley. Leon looked doubtful. Right then, an actual city bus came from the other direction and dropped people off on the other side of the road. A tiny bit of Leon's confidence returned.

This trip was scarier than being on a motorcycle surrounded by drunk drivers. While on that mountain, there were mere inches of clearance between the truck and the cliff. Our cat has never willingly looked out a window again in mountainous areas. People say animals do not have long-term memories, but I am positive that Morgan remembers. That day traumatized him for life.

If Leon was not a good driver, and the traction on the tires was not so perfect, we would have tumbled off, and nobody would have ever found us because no one would have known where to look. We were off the grid.

This experience humbled me. It was scary, but we got through it. At that moment, I knew that if we survived that, we could get through anything. In an instant, we would lose our purpose and value in this world. At those moments, you begin to appreciate even the trivial things in life. It is in those moments that you know the real significance of life and existence.

When you think about it, there is nothing insignificant about life's journey when faced with your mortality. Everything matters, no matter how minute it may seem. When faced with imminent death, you tend to look back at all the moments in your life and realize that it all mattered in one way or another.

THE DAILY GRIND

Just because we were living in Mexico did not mean we did not have to work after all, we were not independently wealthy. Since we were in Mexico on FM-3 resident status, we had to prove to the government that we were not there to work illegally. We had to show that we earned $1,200 a month regularly and had to prove that income came from outside Mexico, which we could easily do because we worked for Evernote.

When we started at Evernote, the company had an office in Sunnyvale, California, on the first and second floors of a dingy, run-down building. The office itself was tiny, and people were perpetually scrambling the desks in an attempt to reconfigure the space. It is hard to believe now, but then we kept the original server for Evernote in the closet in the back of the office.

In late 2008, when we had received our additional funding, we were able to move the headquarters of the company to Mountain View, California, which was around fifteen miles away from Sunnyvale. Our new office space was in a substantial warehouse, so instead of a traditional office where people were crammed into little offices and split onto different floors, the new space was wide open, and there was plenty of room for employees to move around. Although it was much bigger than the company needed at the time since there were only about 20 employees, we were optimistic and planning for the future.

We initially rented out the front part of this space, and we had the option to extend it and knock down a wall and get more space if we needed it. That space would prove to be particularly useful as we grew into a "real" company, but early on, we rented it out to another set of founders, Jan Koum and Brian Acton. They were working on their new messaging app, WhatsApp. We left them to their own devices, as we had more important things to keep us occupied.

As part of our arrangement with Evernote, Leon and I agreed to come to the office a few times a year to ensure we had face time with the other employees and would always be with them for about a week at a time. We were the only ones working support, and when we were working remotely, we were still able to get everything done, so time spent in the office was a time that we were not spending on support. It was crucial, though, for us to spend time in the office to learn about the new things coming out and to provide our input in a way that we could not always give remotely.

These trips were always really exhausting for us because we had to spend a full day in the office, in meetings, and interacting with everyone, and then we still had to go back to our hotel room and work a full day of support. These onsite days would become 20-hour days, so, of course, we got almost no sleep. On top of that, we could only do our travel to and from Mountain View on weekends because that was the only time support was "closed." Travel time, therefore, occurred on our "off" time, but that was part of the price we had to pay for being able to live on a boat in Mexico.

We also felt that we were operating under a set of unrealistic expectations that were established by Phil Libin, the CEO of Evernote. As the only two people at the time to take care of customers, we were under a great deal of pressure to deal with customer issues and questions in a timely and expeditious way. We felt the constant weight of the customer needs, and this was a burden that only we could share. Dave Engberg understood that since he was often working double shifts himself, but it was not the same. We felt underappreciated, taken for granted, and our accomplishments were unrecognized.

Despite how we felt, I made the decision early on that no one would ever see anything but smiles on our faces while we were at the office. We could not sleep, were always buried in work, and the time that we spent there was time we were taking away from our support work, time that we did not have to give. But these problems were not our coworkers', and they did not need to know about our circumstances. Part of our job was to shield the rest of the company from the drudgery of support; we would filter all the feedback, the bugs, and any other issues that appeared and present it in a way that was productive and actionable.

When making these trips, we would generally go from a Saturday to a Sunday since not only did that conform to our work schedule, but also that was when the flights were cheaper. Surprisingly, hotel rooms were also less expensive for more extended stays. As these trips lasted more than a week, it was too long to leave Morgan alone, so he had to come with us. We had to make the hour and a half drive down to Cabo San Lucas from La Paz to get our flights. We chose to depart from Cabo San Lucas because the flights to San Francisco were cheaper than those leaving from La Paz, and they were non-stop.

On one trip, while we were waiting in the airport with Morgan's health certificate readily available, we decided to give Morgan some exercise. We put his leash on him, and we walked him around the airport. Typically, when he was on his stroll, people stopped to take pictures of him. Also, since this was Cabo San Lucas, many celebrities traveled through this airport. People always seemed to think that we were celebrities, too, because we had what looked like a leopard on a leash roaming free in the Cabo San Lucas airport. No one ever stopped us.

It was quite the picture: Leon holding the leash and both basking in the attention. Every time Morgan heard the click of another camera, he paused and posed. I walked away momentarily to get some water, and when I returned, there was a crowd of people around them. Morgan was strutting around and preening, and Leon beamed. When we boarded the relatively empty plane, the flight attendants moved us up to the front so they could sneak looks at Morgan in their "down" time. Even cats can have significance, and if they can bring some meaning to someone's life, consider how much we could each contribute.

Our constant challenge was what to do with him while we were at work. We obviously could not bring Morgan with us, as offices are no place for animals, and cats and cages do not mix. What is even more unusual for a cat is that Morgan hated to be left alone and would cry quite loudly the moment he realized he was alone, and we believe he would not stop until one of us returned to his side. So, while we had to take him with us on trips, we still had to leave him alone in the hotel every day. Bengals imprint on their owners; they love you, and they are so happy to be with you, so much so that if they are not with you, they start to get depressed.

We approached this issue as merely another problem to solve. As our work consisted of answering overwhelmingly negative emails, on the boat, we had gotten into the habit of playing cartoons on the TV. We set the volume low, so as not to disturb our trains of thought, but they were classic cartoons like The Simpsons, Family Guy, and South Park that we knew by heart. With a glance at the screen, they instantly transported us to a state of calmness.

Morgan would usually curl up next to one of us while we were working, and his eyes often were transfixed on the television. Hoping that this "fourth member of our family" would be enough for Morgan while we were traveling, Leon turned on the Cartoon Network (which thankfully was running a Family Guy marathon at the time) on the hotel TV. He plopped Morgan down onto the bed in front of it. As hoped, Morgan's eyes went right to the screen. We grabbed our laptops, slipped out of the hotel room, and when we returned later that day, he was still on the bed watching television. An easy solution—and it gave us one less thing to have to deal with when we were at the office.

SHARK WEEK

Periodically, the entire company would gather and put forward all the ideas that we had for the direction of the product. This time was labeled 'Shark Week.' We brainstormed and voiced every opinion and goal we had, and then Phil Constantinou, our VP of products, put them into a product sheet, like a calendar, for implementation. Those initial ideas became the backbone of the company.

For Shark Week to work, however, these needed to be high-level goals. Phil Constantinou gathered a whole week's worth of ideas from an entire group of people, who then voted on what was most important and what was slightly important. He filtered that by what would make us money and gain new customers immediately versus what would make us money in the long term. We needed to focus on the things that would make us money in a short time, as we would never be able to expand to build long-term ideas without that.

I cannot think of a single idea that we did not eventually implement. We were creating a multi-year plan for the company, and some ideas took the full six years to put into practice, but by doing this early on, it gave an overall structure for development. The company started to come together in this way. We understood that to build something with real significance takes time, and not everything should be. It takes numerous people and many ideas to form something as big as Evernote, and the timing must be right. Not all opinions are equal, and you cannot implement all ideas instantly.

While it may be discouraging for those who do not see their ideas immediately implemented, the reality is you will have priorities and limited resources, especially for smaller companies. There were times when I felt discouraged because they ignored my suggestions, such as offering to save previous versions of people's notes, because, to me, my ideas seemed like the most important of all of them.

At one point, incredibly early on, I was adamant that we make an Enterprise (or Large Corporate) level offering as I convinced myself that was where the company would be able to find its actual customers. I knew that Enterprise certainly was not going to be done overnight, but I was insistent that we focus on the Enterprise customers and their needs. By doing so, we would be able to make the company better overall. I knew from my experience that working with this type of customer led to their increased loyalty, and they would more often than not become a long-term customer. As part of this plan, I wanted to create an import tool to help ease the transition for customers from other products, as well as have some additional features I was sure would appeal to the Enterprise customer. I was confident that we would be able to implement it immediately with a minimum of development effort.

Within my tenure at the company, I got to see all my original ideas implemented. It was incredibly fulfilling and rewarding to see that impact. The real beauty was not *that* things were implemented but in the *how* of their becoming implemented.

I was a significant part of making that happen, not only via my ideas but also as part of a collective community. It was a grand experience to be a part of the process from initial concept, through execution, to the release of a product that is respected worldwide.

That experience paved the way for understanding my life purpose, the living, and breathing of what I love to do every day today. In my current role as an advisor, I help companies understand that there has to be some thought and some planning before their idea is accepted and implemented. That was what we did at the beginning of Evernote. We did not know how we were going to reach our goals since there was no established path laid out for us, merely a dream.

We built Evernote on the thoughts, ideas, and actions of 20 people. We had a combined goal, and then at the end of a "Shark Week," we departed to our respective homes, which were scattered around the country and in Mexico, so we could get to work.

At the end of Shark Week, we peeled Morgan away from his TV, got back on a plane so that we could return to the boat, and then it was back to everyday work. We did have to continue to work double shifts and weekends for the subsequent week to get the support queue back to a manageable state. We were not the only ones working double time, but others might have been able to put something on hold, and we could not. We really could not cut anything back, and I do not honestly think anyone understood that.

I remember Phil Libin at the time telling us that he always forgot that we worked there. He meant it as a compliment, meaning that we were running support so smoothly he never had any problems that he had to deal with from our corner. As a CEO, he always had to put out fires, correct other people's mistakes, and deal with whatever issues that happened to arise. Although I understood his meaning, it was difficult to accept because I felt he did not verbally recognize what we were doing. The fact that he did not acknowledge our work or its significance to me was more than a little distressing because we were working so hard to make this company grow. Leon viewed it differently and always considered Phil's comment a compliment.

I still believe that Phil honestly did not know how much we—any of us—were doing. He could not see all the work we were putting in to build the company properly and to replicate his vision correctly. After all, we were the everyday voice of the company.

The bottom line is that not everyone will identify your significance. People will underestimate what you do and how valuable your contribution is to your organization. You need to know that you are valuable and that your worth and significance exceed your expectations. Sometimes employers know how efficient you are because the work gets done, and when the work always is done, they may have difficulty comparing it to anything else. What they do not know is the sacrifice you put into doing it, the sleepless nights, the loss of time that you could have spent with loved ones, and even those vacation days you could never take.

The truth is, when you are doing what you are supposed to be doing, to others, it may seem effortless, especially when your heart and passion is involved. When you are meeting your needs, the how, the why, and the method becomes almost invisible. That is why it is so easy for others to overlook your significance, but you must never measure your worth through the eyes of others. Recognition should never be your goal for achievement.

When you begin to understand this, you will find that you are always progressing, always growing, and new doors are regularly opening for you. In contrast, others around you appear stagnant and seemingly stuck in the same place for many years. That is significant. When you know your true worth, the right people will always notice, and they will always want you on their team.

Do not label anything you do as insignificant. Every detail counts, no matter how small it is. Keep working hard, and keep pushing yourself beyond your limits, and it will always pay off in the end.

I believe we always are rewarded for our hard work, even when it does not come from the likely and expected sources. I know our significance will not go unnoticed, and we will manage to grow and become more than we ever expected we would.

Essentially, Significance is how you perceive yourself, how much value you place on what you do, and the contributions you make every day.

THE DESIRE FOR SIGNIFICANCE

Billions of people live on this planet, each fighting to stand out and be more than just another face in the crowd. What it comes down to is that everyone wants to be unique.

We cannot help it. We crave the positive attention and the connection we get from our parents when we are children. We try to find that something that we can identify with to make us "stand out" from the crowd, something that says we are rare.

By keeping our need for Significance balanced with our need for Love and Connection, we can keep ourselves on the path to emotional wellbeing.

Here are some healthy examples to fill this need:

LOVE – Love is not only a way to balance your need for Significance but is itself a way for you to feel special and unique. Whenever you are in love or have love, it is remarkable and is different from any other emotion or relationship. Being loved makes you feel significant and heightens your mood.

LEARN – One can gain a profound sense of Significance by becoming a subject matter expert. The more advanced a degree one pursues in a subject, or the more obscure the subject one studies, the more special they will feel as people recognize their unique knowledge.

EARN – Having a position that earns money, and more specifically, being able to buy items that your peers do not have will give some people a sense of Significance.

GIVE – Volunteering your time, donating money or goods, or teaching are all ways that people will be able to gain a heightened sense of Significance. By being able to share things that you feel are uniquely yours, you will feel special.

THANK – By becoming involved spiritually, people gain a sense of Significance. The more they spend time following their personal beliefs, the more unique they feel. Everyone's beliefs are very personal and different and are the ultimate source of Significance.

4.
Love &
Connection

SEGWAYS

There exists a connection between each of the basic human needs. I would not have been able to take the leaps into the uncertain territory without the benefit of certainty. There is a similar relationship between the need for Significance and that of Love & Connection. Finding the balance within oneself and these two needs can be difficult as they are both strong; however, there can be a certain symbiosis if two people form that bridge. And sometimes, by paying attention to one need, another may be filled.

After our harrowing experience with the motorcycle, we decided to sell it as soon as possible. Now, the truck, the boat, and the Jet Ski were our only means of transportation, and two of those were not practical for everyday use. We thought about getting bicycles because many people on boats had folding bikes that were easily stored. Once they would get to a new location, they could simply unfold the bikes, ride off into town, gather supplies, and return.

However, there was a significant problem with this plan. I am not into exercise, or anything having to do with any physical exertion—not even slightly. I am not very outdoorsy, and I do not like the idea of getting myself somewhere without a good plan to get home. For example, swimming laps around the boat was acceptable because the boat was home, and I could get back onto it whenever I got tired, but riding a bike miles away frightened me.

Keeping in mind all those issues, we had to consider what would two people who worked for a Silicon Valley company purchase when they needed to get around locally. We had a modest amount of space and wanted reliable, low-impact, automatic transportation that was not a motorcycle.

The obvious answer was a Segway.

The Segway was an inspiration, a goal, and a dream for me. When I first learned that the Segway was going to be released (I had been following the codename Ginger and "IT" projects for months), I was utterly fascinated by it because it was something unlike anything I had ever seen before. Dean Kamen, the inventor, spoke of it as the transportation revolution of the future. Like all entrepreneurs, he felt this was going to change the world; it was going to transform transportation, so everyone was going to need one.

Kamen had seen the traffic problems in China and India, where pedestrians and bicycles exponentially outnumber automobiles, causing gridlock and often-fatal accidents. He wanted to invent a new mode of transportation, which would relieve congestion, be eco-friendlier, and be a more reliable method of transportation than ones currently in use. Unfortunately, a Segway costs as much as a lower-end automobile, and people genuinely look silly riding one. Kamen failed to spot that critical fact when designing the Segway: no matter how good the intentions, most people will not willingly become a source of amusement for random onlookers.

The first time I saw one in person was in early 2002, at a display in "The house of the Future" at Disneyworld in Orlando, Florida. There was a demonstration of the iBot self-balancing, stair-climbing wheelchair, and the Segway. People could test-ride the Segways on a slalom course they had set up with the option to go on a full tour around the park. From that first moment, when I stepped on it, and I felt the gyros balance underneath me, I was smitten.

Leon observed how happy zipping around on the Segway made me, but like most young married couples, we had very little extra money. We were living paycheck to paycheck, paying our bills, and we did not have money to spend on whims and luxuries. Simply put, we were in debt, and there was no way we could afford a single frivolous item that cost $8000, let alone two of them! If we were going to spend that kind of money, we would spend it on a car.

By 2009, our financial circumstances had changed, but so had Segways. The company turned out to be a colossal failure. Segways did not change the world of transportation. The only people who personally owned them were wealthy Silicon Valley tech people who used them to play Segway Polo. They were people who had enough disposable income to purchase them and use them no more than once a month. Segway's only large-scale customers were security companies and police departments, who used them to go on patrol and tour agencies that used them for novelty "Segway City Tours."

You do not need to be a Wall Street analyst to understand that a company that sells a product with limited appeal and a limited market is doomed. While they managed to keep themselves afloat for longer than anyone expected, they never reached a scale that allowed the price to come down from that $8000 a unit. However, since they had been in use for seven years, a secondary market existed for them, and those used models were within the scope of our disposable income. There was another and probably more important reason for us to purchase Segways at this particular time.

Work was beginning to take a toll on me. I was finding it hard to get out of bed in the morning. There were days when I was back to my old pattern of "wake up, open the laptop, work 12 hours, close the laptop, sleep" without taking a break, without saying a word, without even moving from the bed. Leon grew increasingly concerned, but nothing he said or did seemed to be able to get me to stop working. I would tell him that

I had to keep working until all the tickets were processed. He would sit back and worry because I was taking care of everyone except myself.

Leon hatched a plan. Unbeknownst to me, he started the search for a used Segway. It was a somewhat impractical search at that time since we were deep within the Baja. Still, he managed to find an advertising company in Southern California that was retiring two of theirs because Segway had recently released a newer model. He arranged for the purchase, then made the four days drive up the coast to pick them up and bring them back down to the boat.

His love for me and his understanding of my needs helped him to find a way to feed my Significance. I began to understand that I did not need recognition or accolades at work, and I had started to resent myself for feeling depressed about not getting any. By purchasing the Segways, Leon instantly snapped me out of that.

Every time I got on the Segway, I would smile; I was happy even as I was putting on my bike helmet to complete the geeky looking picture. We would roll out of the marina and into town at a blazingly fast 12MPH, hugging the coast the whole time. While in town, we would do some shopping, go to lunch or dinner, or even walk around and look at the beach. We didn't need to lock them up; we had the keys, and no one knew what they were. Even if someone had tried to steal one, they would have been effortless to find since they were the only Segways in La Paz.

When we parked outside a restaurant, people would ask what they were. There was no way for me to explain a Segway and how to use it in Spanish. So instead, we let people try them out. I got so much enjoyment out of giving Segway rides to people. First, one person, then another, and then another would come over to try out the new kind of vehicle these crazy Americans had.

People started daring their friends to get on, and we all watched as their faces would light up as the machine began to balance under their weight. There was more than one "Woo Hoo!" as a recruit picked up speed down a straightaway or learned how to spin it in loops. We were happy then, and what is more, we were delighted to share that joy with the people around us. Our Segways became a fun community event.

Even as we taught other people how to use them, we often still did not lock them up while out on errands.

We were not rich, even though many in La Paz were. All we had was something that brought us joy, and we wanted to share it. We knew that we were probably the only ones who would ever come through town with Segways, and there was no point in keeping them hidden because, to be honest, there is no way to hide when you're on a Segway. In sharing our joy with other people, we seemed to make their lives a little happier.

I think my happiness also stemmed from a shared experience, not because I had something other people wanted. The residents of La Paz saw beyond the geeky Americans in helmets riding around on Segways. All they saw and experienced was something different and fun. I think if the Segway company had marketed it that way—as a very cool toy—rather than as the end-all solution to global transportation needs, they would have been much more successful.

The price point for a new Segway was always too high, but the secondhand market resolved that issue. I am thankful that we did get to own them. The Segways were a bridge to two of my needs, Significance and Connection. Getting them pulled me out of depression, made me more balanced at work, and helped me to connect with Leon and our greater community. They enabled me to connect on an emotional level with everyone around me and to spread the joy and happiness I was feeling.

TIME MANAGEMENT

This shift in my outlook began to influence my entire attitude toward life and work almost immediately. We were two people, working and living in cramped quarters, somehow not managing to see or speak to each other much, and we now had started to grow emotionally closer to each other.

Life started to be fun for the first time since before we were married. Even though we had the pressures of work, it was no longer drudgery. We respected the power entrusted to us, and it was very fulfilling. Every day we got to deal with something new, as customers would run into a problem that we had not encountered before. We would have to investigate, test, and ultimately solve the problem. Leon would be the first line filter, sending out the responses to things we were already familiar with, or answering questions that would take no more than 5 minutes per ticket. He then sent me anything that would take longer than a few minutes, "teeing me up" as it were. As a result, he would routinely answer over 100 tickets a day, while I would only have between 50 and 80. He would expect me to write new answers to close out those tickets, which he could then send out for cases that came in with similar issues.

Years later, many of the procedures I wrote then are still the answers being sent out by Evernote Support with minor alterations. I spent time making sure I got it right the first time, providing a solid foundation for the support teams that followed. The discrepancy in the number of tickets we would close out was still a cause of disagreement. Even though Leon knew my tickets required me to research answers, he often complained that I would spend too much time on any one case. There were two types of users, Free and Premium. Premium users paid us $5.00 a month or $45.00 a year, and we needed to respond to them within one business day.

In his mind, the Premium users were the ones we were supposed to spend time on, leaving the Free at the back of the queue. My rationale was that it did not matter how long we spent on any of them. If it was in my queue, it was still going to be someone's problem later, Free or Premium, so I might as well spend the time fixing it now.

When you look at the bigger picture, you start to understand things differently. I spent hours attending to the needs of free users that paid off in the long run for the company as a whole. Leon eventually saw that my method worked, and while he was never exactly happy about it, he did lighten up.

THE SEA OF CORTEZ

Although we did work numerous hours, we did not stay docked all the time. One of the reasons we chose La Paz was because of its location in the Sea of Cortez. A four-hour sail brought us into isolated islands as beautiful as any in the Caribbean. We sailed up to a protected cove, anchored out, and lay under a sky full of stars.

I had never before in my life felt like that. I had never felt so connected to life, the world around me, and to another person. I found something in my relationship with Leon that I never knew I had, and I found something in myself as well.

We had an MP3 player hooked up to the boat, and we would pipe music through its speakers. We laid out on the deck for hours, holding hands, singing songs, drinking Pacifico, or sipping Tequila. I had an app on my phone that, when I pointed it at the sky, would list the locations of constellations, so we spent time pointing it at the sky, being silly, and doing things like pretending we could see Pluto with the naked eye.

Some whales came to birth their calves here because it was secluded, and the water was warm. If it was the right time of the year, we could hear them in the water. Sometimes they would surface, and because they were blue whales, all you could see was a little bit of their nose ridge or slight disturbance water to alert you to the presence of this massive creature.

One time, we were lying out, and we saw the ridge of a blue whale directly in front of us. It was dusk, but it appeared to be only 200 feet away. The sky was a beautiful salmon color, and the sea was deep, deep grey-blue when we saw the whale. We were both alarmed and thrilled. We anchored in a cove too small for the whale to enter, so we were not anxious that it would come near the boat, but we knew that there was a blue whale out there.

That was a moment for us, and it was over as quickly as it happened. The whale slipped down under the waves as the stars started to come out, one by one. We had our music playing as the soundtrack to the night, and we were back to lying there, enjoying each other's company, and it was good.

It is within those moments that you learn to appreciate and know what true love is. Those moments were peaceful. There was something about sharing that with Leon that strengthened our connection. Despite all the customers complaining to us all day, every day about their software not working, we derived pleasure and happiness by being together.

Every weekday people were angry, frustrated, and often hostile and nasty, but on weekends we could escape to this peaceful haven only four hours away. We got through each week knowing we were on this vessel that could get us to that place where it was just the two of us. Even today, years later, I long to be on a boat, as it was a refuge where I know can take me somewhere where I can find true peace.

The boat was not only our home; it was a massive part of our lives, a defining source of contentment for us, and a common ground for both of us in our relationship.

That sense of "the two of us" was something I learned to appreciate about boat life that I had not anticipated. On land, there is always someone somewhere, but out on the ocean, the likelihood of that is very slim. The sense of seclusion was perfect, and we loved it. It was so quiet; we could hear the waves lapping up against the boat, and boats are where I get my best sleep. What's funny is I think Morgan is the same way. Whenever we would visit the boat, he would jump out of our arms and run to the boat, where we would see him lounging on the deck, sunning himself before we have even gotten halfway down the dock.

LIFE IN MEXICO

Now that we had struck a work/life balance, we focused on more mundane tasks, like provisioning the boat with our everyday necessities. Leon had decided against moving to Mexico because he did not want to learn Spanish. With tongue firmly in cheek, he declared, "There are millions of Mexicans coming into the US every year refusing to learn English, so I am going to be an American who moves to Mexico and refuses to learn any Spanish."

He steadfastly held to that plan during our years abroad. It amused him to tell people, "I'm going to speak English at people the whole time I'm here. Tit for tat." He did learn a few important words, but for the most part, he refused to speak Spanish the entire time we were in Mexico.

Since we were both working, and we had to go out together, we had to work out the best time for us to get our supplies. It turned out that we could spare a few hours once a week and that generally turned out to be on Thursday afternoon. We withdrew around 6000 pesos a month from an ATM to use as spending money and to pay in cash for everything. Then we budgeted for groceries, boat parts, and other necessities. We figured out our meal plan for the week, and then got everything we needed in that allocated time before preparing for our sailing excursions on Friday afternoons.

You can imagine how this enforced togetherness limited us when there were errands to do, such as buying groceries. Leon could not go alone and would insist that we both had to go. He argued that we were in a foreign country, and so I could not go anywhere without him because he needed to protect me. La Paz was a very safe community, and I felt that I did not need his protection, but I chose not to challenge him. It turned out that doing things together was a big plus for our relationship. I have found that the foundation of many successful relationships.

In most cases, a husband and wife will work separately, have separate hobbies, and only see each other for a few minutes at a time. In our case, we were spending every waking minute with each other, working together, traveling together, and did just about everything together. A friend of mine would ask, "Did you say I do, or I glue?" I must confess, though, that I was getting concerned because our world was getting ridiculously small. I think I lost the ability or interest to do anything by myself.

Our relationship continued to change and evolve. We would go to the grocery store, and I had to read all the labels to Leon because he did not know the language, and he had learned not to trust that the pictures were representative of the contents. Whether it was because Leon was trying to build a more reliable connection with me, or he honestly felt lost, he forced me to take care of him. I had never been in this situation before, with anyone. He was essentially saying that he needed me to take care of him, so I did. It became second nature to me, and I found that I loved doing it. It worked for us. I had no idea that in meeting his needs, I was also meeting my own.

We even got some prepaid cell phones so we could call each other if we were separated and got lost, but we were never more than 25 feet away from each other. I know that this type of relationship is not appealing to many people, but given our circumstances and our love and connection to each other, we thrived, and our bond grew strong. In contrast to this closeness, I remember the early days of our marriage when we were apart for prolonged periods. We eventually settled into a happy medium. During these days in Mexico, we learned to operate independently from each other.

I was the one who could speak the language in Mexico, get our provisions, and cook. Leon liked to fix things and tinker, so that and sailing were his domain. He offered, but I did not even want to learn to sail; he was the captain. He was our sole means of getting around on the water. Our skills were complementary and provided balance. We were not in competition and found that by letting each other do the things that made us happy and giving ourselves the space to do that, our bond strengthened.

Marriages usually begin with the understanding that there needs compromise, and each partner will, at some point, must sacrifice his or her own needs and demands for the other. Often within the confines of the marriage, partners can become complacent and self-absorbed, so the self or ego tends to resurface and assert itself to assume dominance in the relationship and influence the dynamics of the marriage. Eventually, couples tend to lose that initial connection and promise and the love that initially brought them together. What people miss is that no one should have to sacrifice anything. If they simply nourish each other's strengths and build on the connections that they create, the relationship will thrive.

Without taking the time to rebuild the love that was missing from my life and strengthening that connection, I may never have gotten to where I am today.

As someone unknown once said, "Success is nothing unless you have someone you truly love to share it with."

UNDERSTANDING LOVE & CONNECTION

People often write about Love.

Robert Heinlein wrote: "Love is the condition in which the happiness of another person is essential to your own."

Karl Menninger said: "Love cures people—both the ones who give it and the ones who receive it."

And perhaps the most poignant of all, Lao Tzu: "Being deeply loved by someone gives you strength while loving someone deeply gives you courage." This is the basis of the "Need" for Love & Connection. Everyone feels love deeply, both when they have it and when they do not. It goes in two directions, as it requires a person to love and a person to be loved.

We are born with this need first—the need to be loved, to have a connection with another person. Most people need to be loved by someone to survive and take care of themselves.

It is no wonder that this need remains the strongest for many people throughout their lives. Here are some ways you can fill this basic human need:

FAMILY – We are given a bond to a group of other people from our very first moments on this planet. If we spend time with our family members, expanding and growing this relationship, we should have a network supporting and strengthening us throughout our lives.

FRIENDS – Friends are a source of enrichment that you can find at any point in your life. By creating friendships, you can grow with other people and help them enrich their lives as you do yours. You will find that by being someone's friend, you will become the best version of yourself.

TEAMS – Joining a team will allow you to operate in group environments, as opposed to one-on-one. In connecting, you are working together for the good of the whole rather than the good of the self.

PETS – Caring for a pet is a symbiotic relationship—by caring for a living creature, you may gain a sense of accomplishment. People often feel less lonely by having the companionship of a pet.

GIVING – By giving (a gift, a hug, anything really), you are establishing a connection with your receiver. Random acts of kindness, especially, have a positive impact on both the giver and receiver.

Keep in mind that while filling your need for Love & Connection, you have the unique ability to affect the wellbeing of two or more people at the same time.

"Yet now, as he roared across the night sky toward an unknown destiny, he found himself facing that bleak and ultimate question which so few men can answer to their satisfaction. 'What have I done with my life,' he asked himself, 'that the world will be poorer if I leave it?'"

—ARTHUR C. CLARKE, *GLIDE PATH*

5.
Contribution

BUILDING A HOME

Like the other basic needs, Contribution does not stand alone, but this need exists with Growth. These two needs are known as needs of the Spirit, and in some ways, they are a fulfillment of the four physical requirements. Once your physical needs are satiated, you will discover that your spirit soars. You look outward and find that there is more to you than merely your own needs and desires. This sense of giving back to others is what we call Contribution.

It happened so gradually that we were taken completely by surprise when we realized we had turned a corner. The work that we had once described as tedious, frustrating, and filled with drudgery was now *exciting* because we got to help people daily. Those angry customers who used to make us tear our hair out became *opportunities* for us to reappraise negative experiences into positive ones.

Through answering support questions, troubleshooting bugs, coding workarounds, and authoring knowledge-based articles, we were helping people around the world. Not only were we helping individual customers, but we were also contributing to the overall well-being of the company.

No matter our location—sea, land, or air—we continued to lead Customer Service, Account Management, and Technical Support for Evernote, so one of our myriad laptops was always open. We were always working, building, and contributing. We even trained ourselves to get over our motion sickness as long as we were staring at the computer screen. We were able to tune everything out but work and ignore all external distractions. We would put ourselves into "the zone" and get work done—not because we had to, but because it was like a drug calling us back.

Frequently, we would have our customers start conversing with us about their own lives—initially, it would take the form of "I love Evernote—I use it extensively for preserving my grandmother's recipe collection."

It quickly became apparent that no matter what TechCrunch or other Silicon Valley journalists thought, we were not a productivity tool. Customers entrusted us to store their most treasured memories—and as we had learned at CoreStreet, your paying clients ultimately determine the direction of the company.

We had become more than merely a digital extension of an existing product.

Several people had email addresses from Hotmail or Gmail with an automatic signature at the bottom, stating that they had sent the email from a public facility, like a library—something I did not see often. I remember one particular person because it was a troubleshooting case. He started to tell me the usual story about how he "needed" to get his notes back; of course, like everyone else who contacted us, his data was the most essential thing in the world.

Then the story got a bit different. The man said that he was homeless and was using Evernote to save articles for his advocacy for the rights of the homeless. He went to the public library every day or so and logged on to the free computers there, did some research, learned something new, read books, captured the information that he wanted, and stored things in Evernote. As this was the first time we saw this problem, it took us a while to figure it out and get his account fixed. It was during that troubleshooting and trial and error phase that he recounted his story.

"Most of what I've been clipping are articles on the Homeless, and though I am homeless myself have been trying to be an advocate for homeless issues around the country. When I started moving online for homeless advocacy and ministry in November, Evernote leaped out at me as a way to keep track of the issues. I have a laptop I've managed to keep running for six years, but it has crashed more lately, and I'm trying to keep the data stored online or on my three flash drives (512Mb, 2Gb, and 4Gb) so that it is not lost.

"Evernote has allowed me to clip an item and go back to it to reference it in my writings and blogs. Using the sync option, I can do so without having to be online. I've also been encouraged to write a book, which may come much later, but with limited time available online, I can clip a site, sync the Evernote clips to my flash drive, and then view the material later.

"Tonight, for instance, is National Homeless Person's Memorial Day—an occasion on the longest night of the year to remember the homeless in this nation who have died on the streets, mostly due to cold and the elements. While it's a nationwide event, here—where I am at present in Kansas City—not a single agency for the homeless or shelter has ever heard of it, and thus no remembrance will be had tonight."

It was then that I realized we were doing something that touched people. We were making a valuable contribution. Evernote had created a place where people could capture and store their memories; it was a place to put their most precious thoughts and recollections and save them. So, I wrote myself a note that day that read, "With Evernote, you are never homeless. Evernote is the home for your memories. And your memories are the most important and most precious thing you can ever have."

I woke up every morning with that as my mantra. For years after that, if I found anyone who wrote to us who was homeless, I made sure to give that person a free premium subscription, which provided more storage space. During natural disasters like Hurricane Sandy or the Tsunami in

Japan, I urged the company to issue free Evernote premium accounts to the affected people so that they would be able to store their memories, documents, and information. It is an emotional topic for me and sometimes challenging to discuss. Still, it was only the logical evolution of the old entrepreneurial trope, "We were doing this to change the world."

Evernote did change the world, and its contributions far exceeded expectations. This billion-dollar idea did impact lives in a positive and fulfilling way because "You can never be homeless with Evernote."

THE THREE SEASHELLS

As part of our growing responsibilities, Leon and I were in charge of onboarding and training new employees not just for our own department, but for some the international offices. This meant we were often traveling, and this brought us frequently to Zurich, Switzerland and Warsaw, Poland to conduct these training workshops.

Leon and I had both worked at airlines, and both been trained as pilots. When designing our trainings, we therefore decided to model them after traditional ground school, with a combination of lectures, homework, hands-on experience and interactive tests. By this time, we had perfected our training to the point that within one week we could have customer service agents fully skilled in handling any issue, and two weeks for tech support agents. We had a one-day training for any other new-hire to get them familiar with all of the products in the company, which were quickly growing.

At least, we thought we had it perfected.

Part of any good lecture is to ensure you add humor in the right parts. You want to make sure that people are following along, and want to emphasis your points with metaphors that make sense. In other words, you need to tell them a good story so it will sink in. We had many of these built into the training, and it was a key to our success.

One day in Zurich, I was at the head of the room, talking through a presentation on our language translation tool. I had six new employees—one from Germany, one from Switzerland, one from South Korea, one from Russia, one from Taiwan and one from France. Our common language was English, and everyone was following along well, and asking good questions.

At this point, I said a line that always brought a laugh. "While we currently support 48 languages, remember that everything still says the same thing, because in the future, everything is Taco Bell." This time when I told the joke, I got blank stares. Granted, it wasn't that funny, but I didn't get a single chuckle. The woman from Taiwan even wrote down what I said word for word, as if I would test them on it later.

I let it go, but something about it hit me the wrong way. I was "off" for the rest of the day.

That evening, when we were all walking back to the hotel from the office, Torben, the man from Germany, casually started up a conversation about science fiction movies. I was barely paying attention until he said, "Did you know that in some countries, the movie Demolition Man uses a different restaurant chain as the key joke in the movie?"

My ears perked up. I looked at him. He was looking at me with a twinkle in his eye.

He continued. "Yeah, in America, instead of *Pizza Hut*, its *Taco Bell*."

The man from Russia then started to laugh, a big rumbling laugh from inside. "Oh! 'In the future everything is Taco Bell!' Oh, that's funny!" Everyone else started laughing as well, and we started a conversation about other things that might be lost in translation.

I looked at Torben and mouthed, "Thank you." He smiled and swatted the air—"no problem."

POLLO CON PAPAS

In the United States, you purchase roast chickens in grocery stores, and in the Caribbean, they are available from a cart or someone's backyard. In Mexico, you buy roast chicken in a specialty shop called a *Rosticeria*. While out doing errands one day, Leon and I spotted a particularly good looking *Rosticeria* on the way back to the boat and made a mental note to try it later.

On Monday, after finishing all our other errands, we decided that the time had arrived to pick up some chicken. I figured that no one could mess up chicken, and even if that happened, it was only going to be one lunch wasted. I ordered a whole chicken with a side of French fries. As soon as I placed the order, they got out some poultry shears and proceeded to cut the chicken into eight pieces. I tried to stop them, but it was over before I could get out even a word.

When we got home, Leon sat down at the table, opened the package, looked at the pieces of chicken, and stared at me bemusedly.

I shrugged and suggested, "I guess that's how they do it here."

He tore off a piece of chicken from the bone, tasted it, and then absently picked up one of the French fries. He put down the chicken and stared at the fries. I was busy trying to strip all the meat from the bone so we could save the leftovers. When I looked up questioningly, his eyes were wide.

"Stop what you're doing and try these fries," he said.

With hands covered in chicken bits and grease, I reached for a napkin.

"No, leave them," he said. "Just try one."

I did, and they were terrific. We devoured every potato before we had another bite of chicken. The fries were cooked perfectly, not overly greasy or salty—firm on the outside and soft on the inside, and very flavorful.

On Tuesday, Leon proposed that we get chicken again when what he wanted was the French fries. So, we got another chicken, which this time they cut in half, and more French fries—although we now had a cup full of macaroni salad. It was not on the menu, and we had only ordered *pollo rostizado con papas entero*, yet we ended up with chicken, fries, macaroni salad, salsa, and tortillas. Once again, we shrugged and went home. We attacked the chicken, this time saving the fries as our reward for finishing the chicken.

On Wednesday morning, Leon—always planning for his next meal—suggested that we get some chicken for lunch. We could not figure out what they did to the French fries, but we knew we craved them. So, off we went again back to the chicken place. I started mumbling that there had to be another *Rosticeria* closer to the boat. Leon was not interested since he convinced himself that no other place could prepare the chicken and the fries as well. He was addicted to their chicken in only two days.

So, there we were, once more, with yet another chicken, more macaroni salad, another pile of tortillas, more salsa, and yes, more French fries. We did not need more chicken since we had plenty of food from our weekly shopping trip, which occurred on Monday, just before our first encounter with the roast chicken. My very tiny refrigerator was full of our grocery store purchases and the macaroni salad that we were never going to eat.

We could not keep on like that, so I asked the lady in the store what they were doing to those potatoes to make Leon want to come back every day. She smiled, and then simply showed me the location of the potato fryer. It was directly below the rotisserie so that the rotating chicken would drip fat directly into the potato fryer. All of that grease, salt, and the seasoning was going right into the pan. The fat ran out of the chickens and fell directly onto the potatoes, frying all the potatoes in schmaltz.

"We're eating pure fat!" I exclaimed. "That can't be healthy."

"I don't care. They're so good!" Leon replied.

Now that he knew the secret of the potatoes and their fatty origins, he craved them even more. I finally convinced him that we should only have their chicken once a week. Reluctantly he agreed.

On Thursday, I woke up at 1 pm, and Leon was not on the boat, which was strange. He returned at 1:30 and announced that he had a surprise for me. It was an uncut roasted chicken with even more potatoes than before. The man who showed no interest in learning this foreign language had somehow managed to go to the shop and order chicken without the side of macaroni salad. He was pleased with himself and expected me to be as excited as he was. He had solved the problem of the macaroni salad. I was not thrilled.

"We just decided that we were only going to buy chicken once a week. Our fridge is already bursting at the seams!" I cried.

"But this is once a week! We made the decision yesterday, so this is the first day of a new week," he replied, smiling broadly at his reasoning.

The next day I convinced him to eat what we had already bought, along with the leftover chicken that had accumulated. We regrettably tossed the uneaten French fries—which did not taste the same reheated—but we still had two days' worth of untouched macaroni salad.

Our boat mechanic came by the next day, and I always like to offer people refreshments when they visit. Given the early hour he arrived, I did not have anything prepared—so I offered him some macaroni salad.

"Did you say macaroni salad?" he asked. He had a beatific smile on his face. "That's probably my favorite food on the planet—oh, it takes me back. My grandmother used to make it for me back in Ireland, and she'd mix the salad cream just right . . ."

He was elated. He was excited because there was no one in his life now who made macaroni salad for him, and he had such happy memories attached to it. He ate it all—then asked me for the recipe.

"Oh, I didn't make it. It came with this chicken we buy. Would you like to know where we get it?"

"Oh no," he said. "I don't much care for chicken. But that salad is excellent!"

We agreed that anytime we bought chicken, we would save the macaroni salad for him. He came by at least once a week—boats always have something wrong with them—and the salad never seemed to spoil. We would save it, he would eat it, and everyone would be happy. It was a small contribution, but you never know how valuable such gestures can be for the recipient.

GOOD TIMES

I have always found looking at different boats in marinas refreshing. The boats come in all shapes, sizes, and colors—a true reflection of their owners' personalities. Unlike cars, it is rare to see two of the same boat in one marina.

When we arrived in La Paz, we were assigned a slip next to a beautiful 68-foot red and black double-masted ketch named *Halley's Comet* with a pirate flag hoisted up the mainsail. If you tried to imagine what a sailboat should look like, this is the boat you would picture, and we docked right next to it.

We were there a few weeks and had not seen anyone on it, which was not uncommon, as many boats go for months at a time without being occupied or used. I had trouble believing that anyone would let this beauty sit for long. After those few weeks passed, I did hear some noises outside that were the unmistakable sounds of someone provisioning a ship for a weekend trip.

I popped my head above deck and did a double-take because I saw what looked like John Amos, the actor, 10 feet away from me handing bags of groceries onto the deck of the boat. There I was in my pajamas watching this famous actor perform a mundane task. I went below deck quickly and did a Google search, trying to link John Amos with the boat docked next to me.

I learned that Amos, after starring in Roots, Good Times, Coming to America, and many other memorable roles, had started the Halley's Comet Foundation. Their mission statement was:

"We at Halley's Comet Foundation have a very strong conviction that by exposing an at-risk child to sailing, we make a positive and long-lasting change in their outlook. The experience of working at any job as a member of a team can be beneficial. The very nature of sailing requires the utmost in preparation, planning, and teamwork."

John himself also said, "We need to protect the resources and livelihoods, not just the ones we have today, but in the future, too. We have an opportunity to get it right, and that's important to the entire nation." John Amos was a contributor and committed to making the world a better place.

Morgan, not to be ignored, jumped out of his leash and cleanly jumped from our boat to Amos' boat landing at the foot of the woman I believe was Amos' wife. She and Amos looked at Morgan, noticed me, and then said, "What a beautiful cat!" She picked him up and walked him off the boat to hand him to me as I tried to smooth out my pajamas and untangle my hair to look marginally presentable. I mumbled some thanks and quickly disappeared. What had struck me was that of all the boats he could have picked, he chose that one. A ketch is not a forgiving boat, and it is certainly not a pleasure boat. If he were merely a movie star wanting a status symbol, he would have picked something with a motor and bow thrusters. I was intrigued, and I instantly wanted to learn more about this fascinating man.

While both John Amos and I came from the New York City metro area—I from Staten Island and him from Newark, New Jersey, our experiences in life were vastly different. My marina—and every marina, everywhere—was full of people who looked like me. For the children that he founded the foundation to help, that beautiful boat was a symbol of much more than I could ever hope to understand.

What I did understand was that his boat was an example of his ongoing need for Contribution. His work as an actor had provided entertainment to many. However, in his role with the Halley's Comet Foundation, he was using his fame to do something more significant and longer-lasting.

BUILDING COMMUNITY

One of the wonderful things about living in Mexico was that as time went on, we felt comfortable, began to meet people, and connected with others. There was no real language issue in the marina, and meeting new people was not difficult, as we were living in a close-knit community of expatriate Canadians, Americans, Australians, and people from all over the world who also spoke English.

In addition to the marina residents, we found that many of the Mexicans we met had an excellent grasp of the English language. There were very few places we went in our multiple years living there where speaking English was a problem. And this was unexpected. La Paz is not like Cabo San Lucas; it is not a tourist town and is most definitely residential.

Parts of Baja, particularly the Cabo area, can be costly places, and many people, non-residents, and Mexicans had their vacation homes on the Baja. As a consequence of education or employment requirements, most people could conduct a basic conversation in English.

For the most part, we socialized with those in our boating community and with the people who had initially arrived on boats and then eventually bought houses. La Paz was so peaceful that people commonly decided to stay.

There was a local yacht club called *Club Cruceros de la Paz* that we joined. It was a social club that linked all the marinas together. Centrally located to all the marinas in town, the clubhouse was the heart of our expat boating community. Typically, a yacht club is exclusive and expensive to join. Still, this one was 150 pesos for an annual membership, which included a place to have mail delivered, access to the lending library for books and DVDs, and organized activities like bridge, dominos, and yoga classes. It was more like an association where members could mingle than an exclusive club. Once or twice a week, we would check our mail and see what was going on with the other members.

They also broadcasted a radio show that anyone on a boat could hear. It went on air at 7:30 A.M. There were a news and weather segment; a lost and found section; and what I call an anyone, anything segment, which was like a radio call-in show.

I would only half hear the morning show because, at 7:30 in the morning, I was usually still asleep, but I would always be aware of Leon in the other room listening. One morning, someone called in and said that he had broken his computer, and he needed someone to look at it. In my semi-conscious state, I became aware of a few people in a row saying my name and my boat's name. Then I heard Leon grab the radio to tell the person to go to another channel so he could get the details for me. He said that there would be no problem, and he would arrange for me to look at the computer.

That is when I realized that we had successfully integrated into this community: when a random person asked for help, other people pointed to me. People who did not even know or care what the problem was were recommending me; they knew it was a computer problem, and they trusted I would be able to fix it. There were established (Spanish Speaking) businesses in La Paz that could have repaired the computer, but all those people had confidence in me.

I knew that helping people was something I wanted to do, and it made me feel good to know that my efforts were appreciated. Let me be clear: I was not then, nor have I ever officially been a computer repairperson. It is merely something I have always been able to do. It is just natural for me to diagnose what is wrong with electronics and then figure out what is needed to fix them.

This community saw that in me, relied on me, and came to me. I sometimes still get messages from some of them asking if they should install a specific program on their computer or buy a particular piece of hardware—they prefer to consult me instead of wasting money. The power of community and the ability of members to offer meaningful contributions was evident.

In *Outliers: The Story of Success*, by Malcolm Gladwell, he discusses outlier communities and that a significant benefit of building a community is that everyone works together for the good of the whole. You create a thriving community from people who talk to each other, integrate well with each other, learn from each other, have multi-generational dealings, eat together, speak together and, well, care about each other.

What we had in La Paz was a real community where people cared for and trusted each other. Recommendations were earned and not made lightly. In the same way that people depended upon me for my computer skills, I knew that I could recommend my diesel mechanic to somebody halfway around the world to fix his or her boat's engine. As I had proven myself, so had he.

I still miss living there. We were always able to focus on our work, and we knew that if we needed something, we could ask for help, and it would appear. It might take more than one person to arrive at a solution, but that is what a community does. We applied the things that we learned in La Paz to what we were doing at Evernote. We built the infrastructure on that exact premise, building community.

We created a team of support people who had access to everything, but who were also specialists. They learned to depend on each other and to know each other's strengths. That made us efficient because it saves time and effort if there is someone who already knows how to solve a particular problem, rather than having to teach each new person the same thing.

The time I spent in La Paz influenced who I am, my understanding of community, and the importance of contribution. A society of people who work together for the greater good can create something beneficial.

JIMENA

In Cabo San Lucas and the Sea of Cortez, there are not as many hurricanes during hurricane season as there are in the Atlantic Ocean and the Caribbean, but they do come. In 2008, Hurricane Norbert hit, and the devastation was still evident when we arrived months later. In the parts of Mexico we saw, most of the houses were made of cement so they could withstand most storms. But during our scouting mission before moving down to La Paz, we visited one town that had been devastated because, while their cement houses are sturdy, their thatch roofs are not. Consequently, the hurricane had demolished the ceilings, also ruining everything in the homes.

What we realized was that the wealthy lived in cement homes with sturdy and permanent roofs, while many of the other houses used non-durable materials. Additionally, there were not many paved streets, so the roads were all dirt and gravel. One day the town was thriving, and after the hurricane, it was wiped off the map. Everybody who had once lived there had moved somewhere else, leaving a ghost town in their wake. That hurricane had barely touched La Paz, but there was visible evidence of its path in the form of downed trees and some shells of buildings that people had not bothered to rebuild.

Since we were living on a boat, we had to keep our wits about us during hurricane season. We watched the news reports showing storms being named and upgraded with one eye and were busy working with the other. In 2009, most of the hurricanes that season were in the Atlantic, so we considered ourselves lucky—until Hurricane Jimena was upgraded from a tropical storm to a Category 2 Hurricane.

We called Dave Engberg and told him that we did not know what was going to happen, but there was a genuine possibility that we would lose our internet connections. We were concerned about the company because we were the only support people, and we could go dark and be dark for an indeterminate amount of time. There was nowhere for us to go. We could not go to Los Cabos because the hurricane was likely to hit there first. If we were able even to fly out, we might not have a boat when we returned.

That is what it came down to: we could not leave the boat. Staying on the boat was our best option, but if we were going to do that, then we risked going offline, and we honestly did not know how long we would be unable to work. That would spell trouble for the company.

Dave, as always, was efficient and accommodating. He told us that we were doing an excellent job, and if we went down, he would handle it. He would man the queue until we were back online. That one statement both made us feel appreciated and also relieved the stress of knowing that we might not be able to support our customers. He acknowledged that we had not missed a day or missed the 24-hour premium response time since we had started, and he confirmed that he would keep that service going if the hurricane hit us. I am sure Dave will never understand how much it meant to me that he gave us that security when we needed it most.

We gratefully accepted his offer and decided to batten down the hatches and face the hurricane. We made the calculated decision that attempting to drive away on flooded roads was akin to suicide, and being on an adequately secured boat during a hurricane was a lot safer than any of our other choices. The Cabo San Lucas airport was going to be full of tourists needing to get home, and the La Paz airport was full of people trying to leave. We were 1100 miles away from anywhere useful for us to drive; there was simply nowhere for us to go.

If we stayed on the boat, the worst thing that could have happened, once the hurricane had passed over us, would be for us to sail away to somewhere else (provided the mast was still intact). We figured that was our best chance. As the hurricane got closer to us, meteorologists upgraded the storm to a Category 4. Not surprising, almost everyone in all the marinas in town had also chosen to stay, so we took to the VHF radios and started chattering to each other to keep a grim watch throughout the night.

We discussed the progress of the hurricane and received periodically updated radar reports from a local weatherman. To give us something to break the monotony, I started to cook, even though we were not hungry, while Leon sat watch above deck. Other people did the same thing; it naturally turned into that. A sense of needing to help and protect each other in the community emerged, and even the security guards for the marinas did not go home, working a skeleton shift. People pitched in to tie down every boat in every marina, to secure every loose rope. It was methodical, and even as the rain started to beat down heavily, the communities worked together to make sure all boats were secure.

The hurricane hit at 8 P.M.

The first thing I remember happening was the transformer that fed the primary power grid was struck, so all the lights went out. Then we started hearing the sirens, which sounded all night. The traffic lights were out, the power was out, and anyone crazy enough to be on the road got into an accident. Then the streets started to flood, and trees fell. It was a long night, and I do not think any of us slept in any of the marinas in town. We all had power on our boats because we had our generators to provide electricity for us, so the VHF chatter kept going throughout the night.

In the morning, we saw the destruction. For the most part, the storm spared La Paz. It was a category four hurricane, and we managed only to be hit by tropical storm level winds. Branches and trees covered the *Malecon*; a whole building had collapsed. The stores lining the beach had all flooded. Things had washed up on the beach, including some dead animals and fish. It was not nearly as bad as had been predicted, and thankfully we never lost our Internet signal. Even though the power was out, we still had our cellular connection, so that was good.

We soon learned over the radio that things were not so rosy directly south and north of us. In a town called *Muleje*, the storm demolished boats, a man died, and there were places buried under 6 feet of water. A village to the south, called Laguna San Ignacio, was nearly destroyed due to its wooden houses. Reports were coming in from everywhere that not all was well, and that we had been in the eye as it passed, which saved us. In all, 35,000 people were left homeless by this hurricane, with damages over $170 million US dollars.

We were still able to work, but we opted to take half a day so we could help with the cleanup of the downtown area because many people needed help that day. Everyone from the marinas got together and collected clothing, food, supplies, and anything else they could spare. I went through the boat, trying to find something I could donate, but I found very little. There simply is not anything extra on a boat. Surprisingly, I found enough spare parts to build a computer, so I hastily did that thinking somebody could use it. I started making stuff up that I could donate because I felt terrible. The Yacht Club put together a charity fundraiser to help people, and to this day, I still give when they ask for help. There was a real sense of community that I had not experienced since I was a child in New York. I did not think that kind of thing could ever exist again since I viewed the world as a place where everyone was out for himself or herself all the time. I was happy to have been proven wrong.

When you are in the middle of something like that, and you find out what happens when humans band together for the common good, it is a fantastic thing. That is Community, and that is important because without human decency, without the community, there is no point in doing anything. When you take the time to help people, you find yourself growing from those experiences. Every time I gave something away, whether it was time or resources, my character was developing. The change was gradual, and not something I regularly noticed since each action may have produced results so small that they went unrecognized. Then, one day you may wake up and realize you are not the same person you were five or ten years ago. You are better and much more evolved.

That is growth.

LIFE'S CHOICES

After the hurricane, we volunteered to make a supply run to the states as soon as the highway and bridges were clear. There was only one paved highway, and it went all the way from Cabo San Lucas to San Diego. On this route, roughly every 150 miles, there was a military inspection point. These checkpoints are there to find illegal drugs and weapons, and the larger the vehicle, the longer the inspection would take. The lines for the checkpoints would sometimes back up for miles, especially on holidays or after a massive storm like Jimena. It was extremely time-consuming, and we had to go through the inspection process at least six times in each direction of the drive.

Pragmatically, I understood that our truck was a decent size for smuggling things with many compartments for storage, so I did not begrudge them the extra time it took to go over everything. At one of the checkpoints, though, something remarkable happened. As we were pulling up to the inspection point, Morgan, who had been sleeping, woke up, crawled over onto my lap, and then stood up on the window. He used his paw to hit the button that rolls down the window.

Momentarily startled, he jumped back into my arms, but it got the attention of the closest guard on watch. He came over, looked at me, holding the cat.

The guard, who looked to be barely 18 years old, sheepishly asked, "Can I pet him?"

I quickly glanced at Leon. He gave me a shrug, so I gently started to hand Morgan through the window. "Sure, but be careful. He's got very, extraordinarily strong teeth."

The guard shuffled his gun to his shoulder so he could hold him. He had the biggest grin on his face, and he even put his head close to Morgan's—and to my great surprise, Morgan nuzzled against him.

Some other guards came up as well and stroked Morgan's back, all saying how soft and pretty he was. Before I knew it, they had waved us through the checkpoint without making us get out of the truck at all.

At the next checkpoint, when we got out of the truck, we had Morgan on his leash. The drug-sniffing dogs sat by looking at their handlers, unsure as to how they should proceed. Those guards also waved us through quickly, after stopping to pet him for a few minutes. Morgan was becoming our express pass to get through the military checkpoints. We decided that when we were approaching an inspection point, we would pull Morgan from the back seat and put him on the passenger's lap. As soon as we pulled into a checkpoint, we rolled down the window, leaned out with him in view, and prepared for the "Awwwws!" Morgan saved us much time and added sunshine to the lives of those who interacted with him. He was an unusual cat, and along our journey, he helped to expedite many matters. He was a novelty since there were not that many people with Bengals traveling around Mexico.

THE PATH TO CONTRIBUTION

Any act that we perform that makes another person's life better, no matter how small, is one of contribution. A Contribution makes us feel good about ourselves and makes us appreciate ourselves.

Because it is a spiritual need, performing an act of Contribution will fill all our needs of the body at the same time:

CERTAINTY – Being sure of one's ability to Contribute

UNCERTAINTY/VARIETY – The opportunity to give of yourself to different people, or those with diverse needs

SIGNIFICANCE – Feeling unique for having something worthy to give

LOVE/CONNECTION – Creating a connection in the giving

Here are some examples of Contribution:

DONATE – No matter your status in life, by giving whatever you can spare to people who are not as fortunate as yourself, your sense of general well-being will increase. A donation could be your spare change, old clothes, new toys, or even extra toiletries purchased at a buy-one-get-one-free special. Trust me on this: someone will appreciate whatever you give.

VOLUNTEER – Volunteer wherever you feel you can give the most value, whether it is at a nonprofit, a school, a church, a recreation program, or for an individual. Volunteer to hold the door for someone, or to bake cookies for your coworkers. Even the smallest act will increase your well-being.

TEACH – Whenever possible, teach others what you know. You can help further knowledge or shape the opinions of people by sharing what you know and what you have learned with the world.

VOTE – If you are part of an electoral process of any kind, no matter the outcome, it connects you to something greater than yourself. The result could not have happened without your and others' participation.

SUSTAIN – By being ecologically conscious, we can feel that we are leaving the world in a better place than we found it. By composting, reusing any bags, recycling any available materials, and using alternative energy sources, we can attempt to give the earth back some of its lost vitality.

By performing at least one act of Contribution daily, you will find that you are happier, healthier, and more productive.

"The true measure of a man is
not his intelligence or how high he
rises in this freak establishment.
No, the true measure of a man is
this: how quickly can he respond
to the needs of others and how
much of himself he can give."

—PHILIP K. DICK,
OUR FRIENDS FROM FROLIX 8

6.
Growth

SNAPSHOTS IN TIME

Growth, in the spiritual sense, is a need you can fill every day of your life if you are open to it. There is no shortage of growth opportunities in life, and everything can become a learning opportunity. Like individuals in their daily personal and working experiences, entrepreneurs also try new things, make mistakes, learn, and move forward.

From the very first leg of our journey into Mexico, we found many growth opportunities. No sooner had we celebrated solving our customs issues than we were brought down by the realization that we had forgotten to bring food for our cat, and it was Morgan we used to get through customs. From that initial understanding, we realized we were growing as individuals, as a couple, and as part of a company.

Like all developing entities, Evernote grew and changed. In the beginning, Evernote had a small, cramped office in Sunnyvale, CA. We kept the first four servers—shards, as we referred to them—in a closet on the second floor, with the research and development team located downstairs. As a remote employee, I had no desk. I had to work out of the conference room—and get kicked out whenever Phil needed to take a private call or meeting.

In 2008, we moved to a larger office in Mountain View, California. By this time, the staff had almost doubled in size—to 25. We were expanding the team like mad—every department except Marketing and Support went on a hiring binge.

On each successive visit to the office, roughly every three months, we greeted the employees as if *we* were the new hires. This became a running gag. Every time Leon and I visited the office, the newest employees treated us as if it was our first day. The veteran employees viewed this exercise as a hazing ritual for the new people to see how long it took them to figure out we had been there longer than almost anyone else. Then they observed the looks of comprehension and then abject horror for their faux pas on the newbie's faces.

At a later visit, we were about to knock down the back wall so the company could expand its physical presence and take over the next part of the office. By the time we returned, the wall was down, and the number of employees had doubled again. It was like we were viewing a growing company through time-lapsed photographs.

While initially funny, Leon and I soon realized that our anonymity could be a problem. If people did not know who *we* were, then the other remote employees who were less communicative and active would be entirely ignored. A considerable number, roughly one-third of the company, was not located in the headquarters.

We were "attached" to the headquarters, but we had made the conscious choice to live elsewhere. Many people, therefore, knew us only as names on an email list. They "knew" who we were—in a general sense—since we were one of the first groups mentioned in the new employee orientation sessions and materials. At some point, everybody had to deal with support in one way or another, so we were known by reputation by just about everyone, but by 2010 we knew very few employees personally.

Senior engineers knew who we were because we were the ones filing the bugs they needed to assign. Marketing knew us because it was their responsibility to notify us of new developments so that we could inform the customers. Finance knew us because they were the ones paying us.

Our solution was to implement a companywide social media tool called Yammer. Until Yammer existed, very few people could put a face to a name, but once we started using Yammer, there was a complete shift: we were no longer anonymous and faceless. Everyone knew who we were.

It was my goal to support not only the customers but the employees as well. I wanted to ensure that I was valuable to them, and by doing that, I was also helping to build the worldwide community of employees by making the remote employees feel that they, too, were part of the overall team. It was gratifying to see the company grow and to realize that we helped contribute to that growth. It was important to us that our coworkers knew about our contributions to Evernote, and we were able to go from being anonymous to being known.

We were always aware of our unique work environment and had to be flexible and efficient to make it all work. Our entire internet was wireless, so we were using either Wi-Fi or cellular for our connection. Out of necessity and to be responsible, we had three different backup internet sources. We were not going to let anything knock us offline.

ELEPHANT SPOTTING

As the office was growing, so was our user base. We had inherited 5000 users from our initial acquisition of the company from Stephan Pachikov in 2007, and by 2009 we had over 1 million active users. By 2010, we had hit 5 million users, and there were no signs of slowing.

When EverNote launched, it was a Windows-only program. Cellular phones were limited to Blackberries, Windows Mobile Phones, and some other less popular proprietary products. There was no unifying application for them—and to synchronize your data from phone to computer was a tedious process. Generally, if you had any data you wanted to transfer from your phone, it involved a complicated procedure that took a fair amount of time and was barely worth the effort.

Then came the iPhone, and it changed everything. With its promise of applications running on a single cloud server and a platform that could easily connect to your Apple machine, it was easy to see why software developers were rushing to create apps for this new system. We knew that once people understood the benefit of this phone, they would be ditching their clunky old devices in droves and never looking back.

And yet, while we knew our users were out there, based on sales, support volume, and active users, we had not found anyone outside of our circle of friends who had heard of us.

The lack of fanfare became somewhat disheartening.

Rationally, we knew that 5 million people out of 7 billion is a ridiculously small percentage—but emotionally, we desperately wanted to meet these people who were using our product. There was a much higher chance of the employees around our Mountain View office to meet a user, being in the "tech center" of the world, but we still held out hope that we'd find someone, somewhere, in the world that we didn't know who was using our product.

We called this "Elephant Spotting."

Each day, more people would report "Evernote spotted in the wild" on Yammer. They would have noticed someone taking notes on their phone in a coffee shop in San Francisco, or taking a voice note on the train, or using Evernote on their laptop on an airplane.

As we started to send out more T-Shirts and stickers for marketing promotions, employees would post pictures of Evernote stickers seen on laptops, people wearing Evernote t-shirts, and other displays.

The surface area grew wider and wider, until one day we noticed a trend. We had long been tracking the geographic data of our application downloads, and suddenly there was a spike of downloads in Japan. As Evernote was an English-language application, with no marketing or advertising to speak of, this was unusual.

We started searching everywhere we could look for an explanation. The best we could determine was that a Japanese influencer visiting the

Bay Area had heard about us and then told their friends about us. To capitalize on this, we decided to send Phil on a plane to Japan right away and further fan the flames of interest.

It worked.

Within days, the Japanese downloads increased even more and then started to spread west across Asia. From my Mexican vantage point, it was like watching a map of the world light up as more people began to hear of us, one country at a time.

Soon, when I was at the grocery store in La Paz for my weekly shopping run, I saw something that made me do a double-take. In the checkout line ahead of me was a woman with her iPhone, open to an Evernote checklist. As she was placing items on the belt, she was checking them off one-by-one.

I excitedly turned to Leon and started pointing in her direction. He looked at her, and with a massive smile on his face, whispered into my ear, "Good spot. Go post it!"

BIG IN JAPAN

At the time, our team consisted of former EverNote employees acquired in the merger—mostly Russian R&D guys—and CoreStreet people who had been willing to make the jump to Phil's next business. None of us had any background in Japan beyond a basic spoken vocabulary, a love of sushi, and familiarity with anime.

Phil's first visit to Japan brought us attention, but if we wanted to sustain that momentum, we would need to close some local partnerships—people who understood the market.

Luckily, the cult-like following we had begun to cultivate stateside followed us overseas, and we got some attention in high places. Executives at Sony, Canon, Fujitsu, DoCoMo, and others were all interested in hearing what our plans were for the market and had some ideas of their own.

Within a few short months, we had landed deals with many of the top Japanese technology brands to create, well, *something*. In each instance, Evernote would be involved, but we might have to do something customized to make it stand out. We would figure out those details later—for the moment, we had brand recognition and a foothold in Asia.

As we were beginning to develop a Japanese language version of Evernote and brainstorming what the killer "Japan-specific feature" would be, our daily usage in the region remained relatively flat—it was still high, but there was no growth. Whenever we appeared in a news report, the downloads temporarily spiked, but then would dip back down to the high average.

We started to examine the culture and how people were using their devices, as well as what we had available with the existing technology. It turned out that at the time, the cellular network in Japan was much faster than the rest of the world's—the equivalent of our broadband speed today. Therefore, while we were only just experimenting with photo notes in the US, we could take live video notes in Japan.

To make that happen, however, we would need more than just a localized version. We would need people on the ground for testing, development, and support. It seemed like it was time to open a local office. And to our great fortune, the former marketing director from Apple Japan wanted to come aboard and run it.

After many rounds of interviews, I found two candidates to staff the Technical Support and Service departments and brought them over to Mountain View for their orientation. In turn, they would train the rest of the Tokyo office on Evernote brand, culture, products, and services. This "train the trainer" mentality worked well for all of our offices and allowed us to reach the maximum number of people in the minimum time.

Once we trained the whole office, we were ready to release the Japanese language version. We instantly saw an increase in downloads where Japan became 15% of our overall worldwide usage—and stayed there. The staff was busy, morning until night, taking requests for press interviews, sales calls, and even feedback—but not many bug reports.

As error-free code is statistically impossible, we asked our Japanese staff what they thought was the problem. Their answer was, "Oh, it is improper to complain. Better for them to ignore it and for you to fix the problems without them mentioning anything." As Silicon Valley software developers, our philosophy is that a bug does not exist until someone tells us about it. This particular cultural issue was going to be tricky.

Leon and I conferred on this and then tasked the head of Japanese Technical Support to spend one hour per day testing the product, every day. As a new job requirement, we asked him to report every defect he found, no matter how small or seemingly insignificant. In this way, we would capture all the bugs, and no one would break impropriety.

Everything was going smoothly, until one morning, I awakened to my Twitter feed blowing up with news of a tragedy. A Tsunami had hit Japan, causing a meltdown in the Fukushima nuclear reactors and leaving over 300,000 people without homes. Nearly 20,000 people were dead or missing.

My mind and body froze. I kept flipping through the videos of the disaster and reading the posts of people asking for help or reporting the damage. Before I knew it, tears were streaming down my face in a rapid burst.

Leon mobilized immediately—he had seen me in this state before and did not want me to spiral again. He took the laptop away and said, "So, what are we going to do about it?"

His words shook me back to the present moment. "What do you mean? What can *we* do?"

"Lots of things. We can send money to help. We can hop on a plane and look for survivors. We can pick up anchor and start sailing over there. But that's only going to help a few people—what about helping as many as possible?"

I still was not following him. I was in shock.

He continued to gently prod, "We have this product that people around the world use for their memories, their important documents, photos, and everything else they can think of. It seems that there are a bunch of people over there that might have lost everything—but maybe we can give them someplace to document what they have left."

I smiled through the tears. Leon was showing me how with our simple note-taking software, we could change the world on a mass scale—and not just in the boardroom. I reached out and kissed him, then got on the phone.

We decided to make Evernote Premium free for one year to everyone in the affected region in Japan. We would not make any public announcement because we did not want to gain any publicity from the tragedy. It would merely notify anyone who logged in of their new Premium upgrade status. We felt it was the right thing to do.

Word did spread throughout Japan, and it raised our usage numbers and sales tremendously from then on. The goodwill we garnered brought us additional investment and growth throughout the whole region.

T-SHIRT FACTORY

Now that we had evidence that our guerrilla marketing tactics could work, we started to think of other low-cost strategies that could help similarly grow our brand recognition. The cheapest options were anything we could do for free—i.e., with no cost beyond the manpower time of our existing employees and any volunteers.

We came up with a few ideas right away. First, we would set up an affiliate program, where our existing users could earn free months of service by referring others. While commonplace now, it was a relatively new idea at the time for online software. It worked moderately well for us, and we saw an increase in signups right away.

The next thing we did was start looking for partners, where we took a multi-faceted approach. We could run advertisements within our desktop software, and we offered sales of that ad space to relevant partners—with the additional offering of a Paid Upgrade for our customers to remove ad banners. Again, while this seems obvious now, it was revolutionary at the time.

An alternative partner approach we took was to locate distributors with large mailing lists and give them discounts to their membership. One such popular promotion we ran was through the site AppSumo, where we offered a limited Lifetime Membership to Evernote Desktop for a ridiculously low price. All of us in Support were secretly thrilled whenever we had someone who had gotten in on the AppSumo deal contact us for help throughout the years, and we referred to them as the "Rockstar OGs." These accounts ended up costing the company more money than they brought in, but the loyalty of those customers is priceless.

The most lucrative partner approach by far, however, was by working with hardware manufacturers to get our software designed for and added to their operating systems directly—or at least launched in their app stores. Our diligence here enabled us to be in the Apple Store when it first began and be a top recommended app for every device under the sun. We also built partnerships with companies like Moleskine, LiveScribe, Fujitsu, and others, which gave us a broader reach into traditional retail—far beyond a simple software product.

Those relationships take time to build, however, and it can be years before you see results. In the meantime, we needed to do something that would get us noticed right away. Like many startups, we thought it would be a clever idea to print stickers and t-shirts with our logos on them. We would have our employees wear them and hand them out as gifts at meetups or for other promotional type things. Because our logo, a stylized elephant, looked especially good on a t-shirt, and we were fast becoming known as a "cool" company, there became an increased demand for products.

Soon, the shirts proved too popular for us to just give them away for free—even though their only purpose was to advertise our company! We started to create new logo designs in assorted colors and styles and offer them for sale on our site. This tactic worked so well that customers started contacting us with their design ideas. Some of them were so amazing that Andrew Sinkov and Ron Toledo, our marketing team, came up with the idea of running a T-Shirt Design contest in a new area that we were about to launch so that we could build viral interest in Evernote. The winner would have their shirt printed and available in our store, and we met our goal of free advertising. It worked so well that we ran this contest in a few other countries over the next few years.

Later, this morphed into our "Evernote Market." Like all of the products we released, including back to our CoreStreet days, we always started with a small experiment and then chose to expand where we had found initial traction in market research and customer sales. While it seemed to the outsiders that the Market was a strange decision, it was born out of those early product partnerships and t-shirt sales.

CONFERENCE SEASON

As our customer base became substantial, we realized that the number of individual customer meetups that we were holding around the world was fast becoming unsustainable for the few of us that managed the community. I was able to hire a Community Manager who would bridge the ever-growing Support and Marketing teams, and we were starting to translate our online forums and all other marketing materials into multiple languages.

In short, we were getting too big for our startup roots. During a company all-hands, Phil announced that we should have a conference that rivaled Apple's WWDC. He envisioned our team leads walking across a vast stage, explaining all the neat new things that we would have available in the product in the coming year, and offering our partners exhibitor booths.

We held the first Evernote Trunk Conference at the Concourse in San Francisco, and it was a three-day affair, with workshops, breakout sessions, and roundtables. Like every other Silicon Valley Conference, other than Phil's CEO keynote, though, the only thing that anyone cared about was the Friday night party—so that needed to be perfect.

It would be the first time we brought our employees, our business partners, and our customers all together under one roof. We wanted something memorable—and decided to go with a "circus midway" theme as a tongue-in-cheek reference to our Elephant mascot. We had pinball games, skeeball, and other midway games, plus caramel apples, cotton candy, and tons of popcorn and candy available. There was a photo booth and open bar, and each of the carnival games gave tickets to win prizes from our Sponsorship partners.

While the conference and party itself might have seemed indulgent, it was valuable to us on many levels. It gave the people who attended a special feeling and memories that they spread in more word-of-mouth advertising for us. Our business partners got to see first-hand the enthusiasm of our customer base, and they even got instant feedback on the upcoming features we were planning to release. In only one event, we got more value than from the 50 small meetups we had held in the past quarter. We decided that we would continue to run conferences as long as it made financial and business sense.

LIFE'S CHOICES

As the technology industry was growing as fast as Evernote, we were soon bringing more and more things with it on our trips back and forth to Mexico. We decided it would be prudent to purchase an RV to attach to our truck. Once we had that, Morgan's influence was needed more than ever as now we had a vehicle the size of a semi-truck when going through the Mexican military checkpoints.

There was one occasion where Morgan's cuteness was not enough to whisk us through the VIP line. I was walking outside the RV with Morgan on his leash. He was happily playing with the drug dogs when an Inspector marched into the RV. He looked roughly 16, with his chest puffed out to make him look older. He spoke with a falsely deep voice in rapid Spanish to a confused Leon, who had followed him closely behind.

The inspector started opening every cabinet and door in the RV. As they were empty—we were returning from La Paz after a supply trip—he looked flummoxed. When he finally opened the refrigerator, he found a case of Red Bull and not much else—but Leon always stocked up on caffeinated beverages when going on long journeys.

"What is—Red Bull?" he asked.

Leon explained, "It gives you energy." He mimed his hands on a steering wheel and then falling asleep. "Would you like one?"

Leon took one of the cans out of the refrigerator and offered it to the inspector. The young man took it, opened it, and sniffed at the chemical-fruit smell emanating from the can. He smiled, nodded, and said something in Spanish that we did not recognize, then drank the whole thing in one long gulp. He then handed the empty can back to Leon and walked out the door. The inspection was over.

From then on, we traveled with Morgan <u>and</u> extra cases of Red Bull—just in case. We did not want to jinx anything, and we were always well-liked at those checkpoints.

Something similar happened whenever the Coast Guard inspected us on the boat. I always kept a batch of cookies available and would brew coffee or tea, then offer the cookies and coffee while they were filling out their inspection paperwork. I was taught at an early age to be kind, show respect, and allow people to do their jobs. The greatest gift I could give to that person was to show them respect for what they did.

The coast guard and the military officers at those checkpoints were simply doing their jobs, and we respected that and did not try to give them a tough time about it. We had to go through these inspections several times a year, and at one point, we became so well-known that when we got to a checkpoint, we ended up spending more time showing the cat around to all the guards than if we had simply gone through the routine of being checked and searched. The people in line behind us likely were not too happy about it, but we looked at it this way, we were bringing joy to those who served, and in turn, they then would spread that joy to others. It is not always easy to invest some extra time in people, but it always pays off.

One thing that I have always believed is that something as seemingly random as what kitten you picked out of a litter could turn out to be the thing that makes all the difference later in life. I honestly believe that we are the total of all the decisions we make in our lives and that nothing we have ever done, no choice we have ever made is meaningless. Every decision has consequences and lessons to be learned that bring us to today.

Everything you do gets you to where you are on your journey. There is no external force that has done this to you; no one is controlling your life but you. Outside forces can and will influence who you are and the circumstances of your life, but your life is not solely made up of things being done to you. Instead, your actions and choices concerning the outside world make up your life. Your growth is determined by only one thing: you. In essence, you are what *you do.*

A hurricane is not what shifts your course; it is the choices you make because of a hurricane. When the category four hurricane was heading our way, we made specific choices. Those choices affected our lives. While we made decent choices based on the data we had, our jobs could have been in jeopardy if we had not had positive past performance and trust built up with our careers. Our prior actions and our decisions shaped our life.

A substantial cause of dissatisfaction and suffering is that people build their lives on excuses, and they never experience any growth. A passive person will never grow, but if you learn to make choices and act on them, you will never be submissive, but always evolving. Every one of our experiences has contributed to our growth.

Eventually, I became what I do.

Bo Bennett encapsulates this perfectly in his quote; "Those who improve with age embrace the power of personal growth and personal achievement and begin to replace youth with wisdom, innocence with understanding, and lack of purpose with self-actualization."

LEARNING TO GROW

Growth, being a Spiritual Need, strengthens each of the needs of the Body. As we grow, our capacity for all of our other needs grows in proportion. Because of this, you will find that your needs will shift over time to allow for new experiences to influence your development.

To do this, our need for Growth directly influences our need for Contribution. As we grow internally, we have a stronger desire to give back that which we have learned.

Here are some examples of Growth:

EXERCISE – By performing the discipline of repetition required in physical activity, you will feel your body grow strong. Improving your health will also have a positive impact on your emotional well-being.

LEARN – Expand your mind by studying a new skill, a new language, composing music. Go to a museum, read a book, or see a play. Watch the world news. The brain has a nearly unlimited learning capacity, so by continuing to exercise this muscle, you will have an equality unlimited capacity to grow.

IMMERSE – Sometimes, the best way to grow is by submerging yourself; as in swimming, the best way to test what you have learned is by tossing yourself into unfamiliar waters. You eventually will find that you do know how to swim. Likewise, by surrounding yourself with new cultures and experiences, you will soak them in until they become a part of you.

ACHIEVE – If we set achievable goals for ourselves, then we will get into the habit of moving forward. Each time we achieve something, the next target will come easier. It is merely another form of exercise, allowing us to grow to the next level.

CELEBRATE – One of the hardest things to learn in any stage of development is the knowledge that it is essential to celebrate your victories. Real growth happens when you can accept every achievement with humility; you will be a happier individual if you give the proper respect to each "win," whatever the size.

Always remember that you have the ability and the potential within you to grow physically, mentally, and spiritually every day of your life.

7.
Certainty

PANAMA

Certainty was a challenging goal for me to achieve, given the fact that I was working for a startup company—which is always an uncertainty in itself—and our living situation was not traditional. However, neither Leon nor I have ever had a compelling need for certainty, and we found our stability in each other. We were each other's constant during those precarious times. No matter where we were and what we were going through, we were together. Life was good.

Living in Mexico and working at Evernote was a unique lifestyle. As the company started to get bigger, we started to have an increasing number of exciting challenges. In the six years we were at Evernote, there was not a single day that work was not somehow involved.

Since we were initially the only two people handling support, the workload became stressful reasonably quickly. We did everything we could to manage it, but it seemed like everything was a race.

Rationally, we knew that if we worked faster, we would get our work finished sooner, and then we would have more free time to spend together. On the other hand, we had chosen to give up free time so that we could catch up on the work that was piling up—all those extra things that seem to need doing when you are building a company.

It was around this time that we started to have a mantra: "Head down, do work."

Leon became convinced that the more of ourselves we put into the company now, the more money we would earn eventually. He threw himself wholeheartedly into his work.

And there was plenty of it. There were always more Premium user's support tickets to address or new bugs in the software to test and file away. A new product release to write a training guide and new marketing campaigns driving interest to the forums or contact forms—or some other random occurrence to throw off our carefully calculated plans.

No matter what the cause, the result was inevitable; we would have to spend more time working, more time coping, and less time doing "us." Eventually—and not soon enough—the realization set in that we would have to hire people.

As we were still a small company, we were initially afraid to go to Dave and ask him for resources to hire someone. However, we felt we had a reasonably compelling case in our favor:

1. We lived on a boat that could sink in the ocean.
2. We had been through one hurricane already, and there was a possibility that more would appear.
3. The highway system in our area was hazardous, both from other driver's and its remoteness.
4. We were a "single point of failure."

In other words, we had an infrastructure where if either one (or both) of us were hit by a proverbial—or literal—bus, no one could replace us and our knowledge. This disaster would result in unthinkable damage to our business. If we wanted any hope of taking time away or being able to grow, we would need to build out an infrastructure to scale ourselves.

We committed to fixing that problem sooner rather than later so that there would be no uncertainty for Evernote. Even to do something as simple as taking a vacation, we needed to create a structure that could sustain our leaving for *any* length of time. We made sure that we built one strong enough for us to go away *entirely*, and in doing so, we were secure and confident that we could take a 19-day cruise.

In building out the Evernote support team, we anticipated what was needed to support the customers in the future. We manually created an Excel chart of the number of Customer Service tickets that came in each day. This sheet included the number of Technical Support tickets and Forum posts that come in, and we calculated roughly how many each of us answered per day. We then had a rough estimate of how much a Senior, fully trained tech at full speed would be able to handle and were able to create a basic hiring projection. Coincidentally, we used this same chart for all our hiring going forward.

Once it was approved, our initial plan was to hire and train someone so that we might have *some* time off during our vacation. After a long search, we hired a team in India, taught the first employee remotely, and then decided to cruise through the Panama Canal. Dave found this humorous—it amused him that two people who lived on a sailboat would want to take a cruise. For our part, we loved boats so that we would feel right at home. What was exciting to us was that we would wake up each morning in a different place, with someone else to do the cooking, cleaning, and laundry. Heaven!

In preparation for our vacation, I wrote a program that allowed us to connect to the support server, grab all of the new and updated tickets, download them so we could work on them offline. I would then connect again to upload our answers and send them out quickly. In this way, we would only have to connect to the costly cruise ship internet for very brief periods, which was available all the time we were not in port. We could use Wi-Fi or cellular service in port, but that was not necessarily reliable, and I wanted to make sure I could secure the transfer.

For no more than 15 minutes a day, we were able to get all of the information needed up and down; then, we were able to work offline throughout the day as we felt like it. We could easily read the questions, do the testing we needed, and answer the tickets because, typically, none of that required internet access. All of the cards were either questions that we had to analyze, debug, test, and create a procedure (or write code) to answer (which would take hours), or they were things that we already knew the answers to, which took only minutes to answer.

This preparation gave us the security and certainty we needed to allow us to finally take a working vacation, a 19-day cruise through the Panama Canal. In those 19 days, we worked a half-day every day. We wanted to keep some semblance of our typical work pattern, only in a different location. The only days we did not work were the two Saturdays we went on full-day excursions, which helped to recharge us for the week to come.

By taking half days, we finally got to have some time to ourselves. We had vastly different sleeping schedules and interests, so I might have gone off to play bingo or trivia or something like that while Leon was working, or he might have gone off to hang by the pool while I was working. We did not have a pattern to our "off" time because we never shared all the same interests. We did not feel there was a need for us to spend every waking moment together because when we were together, we started working or talking about work. I have never met anyone else who understands the synchronicity we achieved by living and working together for so many years. Whenever I tell others my story, they always wonder how we did that for six years, and my answer is still essentially the same: it was what we wanted to do, and so we did it.

FAILING FORWARD

Before we took any step or made any move, we looked ahead to the future and saw where we wanted to go, then we were able to see what was needed to get there, and it became as simple as putting those things in place. Even when we were not on the same emotional level, we still functioned on this analytical level, until one day we were working like a well-oiled machine. Careful analysis and planning were how we approached everything. Before we moved to Mexico, we put the structure together to make a move, first by scouting the perfect location for us, then by getting all our paperwork in order, right down the line until actually arriving at the dock in La Paz.

Our careful planning and preparation gave us the certainty needed for us to live our uncertain lifestyle. People talk about having charmed lives, being in the right place at the right time, and luck. In our case, luck had nothing to do with it, beyond those "chance" meetings that were Phil's job to work so hard to create.

As a result, the Evernote team was very prepared; we calculated everything we did. What other people refer to as *luck* was our ability to recognize opportunities that were there and react quickly. As with most things in life, if we had made a different choice, the results would have been different. I think our skill was that we recognized what we needed to do and immediately acted. For me, the only way I would be able to accomplish anything was just to knuckle down and do it, and so I seized each new goal with wild abandon.

As very goal-oriented people, we were always striving to accomplish our objectives, whether it was for work or in our personal lives. My approach to everything was to define the problem or the goal, specify out the desired outcome, and then determine how to accomplish it. That approach is a large part of what it means to use Evernote. It is certainly not a coincidence that the highest number of early adopters of Evernote were those who were highly motivated to get things done quickly and efficiently.

Sometimes stopping too long to weigh the pros and cons of certainty and uncertainty can cause someone to get stuck in the rut of circulating thoughts that never convert into action. You should approach life from a completely unfamiliar perspective. There is a methodology that involves every task that you do. You need to determine the most efficient way to get things done and how to achieve an inbox of zero. It is critical to learn how to attain and maintain an uncluttered mind. Do not think about what you want to do; just do it.

Leon and I were able to recognize exactly where we had opportunities and knew when to take advantage of them. As we went along in life, there were indeed points where we could turn around and quit, leave, or stay mired in uncertainty. I know exactly where those points were as clearly today as I did then, but just like with the motorcycle, the truck going through the valley, and the hurricane experience, we kept going. Whenever we encountered new challenges or unfamiliar problems, we never once thought of stopping.

We were never deterred by what we faced. I genuinely believe that there is nothing that I could not handle, and it is my experiences and the challenges I have encountered that have gotten me to where I am now. Part of my knowledge and strength comes from age, but I believe that the major influences were those experiences and situations where decisions were critical or where I had no choice but to sink or swim. Unfortunately, I see too many people who are too sheltered; they do not take that leap for fear of getting hurt. And if they do, they have somebody running up behind to pat them on the back, handing them a trophy for merely participating.

That is not acceptable; it stunts growth because you need to have that point where it is all or nothing. Life is not composed of successes based on the theory of "A for Effort." You either succeeded, or you failed, and if you failed, you need to figure out why you failed, and then dust yourself off and get going again. Never stop in the valley of failures, or you will end up living there. You need to understand that the trail out of the valley always leads to the mountains, and very often, there is only one way out.

Entrepreneurs often hear that they are only as good as the number of failures they have had; that is ridiculous. I agree that it can be beneficial to fail sometimes because that experience could help you succeed later, but you should not be tallying the failures. It should never be about the number of failures you had; instead, it is what you learned from those failures that are important. If the failures in and of themselves were the point, then we would never create anything.

Marie Curie died of radiation poisoning because of all the research she performed understanding X-Rays. In attempting to prove that X-Rays were not merely a theory, she discovered the radium isotope. Curie failed to patent her discovery and ended up sacrificing her life to no financial end. She died from sickness due to prolonged radiation exposure, something she was unable to foresee. However, today, we have her to thank for the life-saving X-Ray machine. Her research and subsequent failure to patent her findings enabled industrial growth that would not have happened otherwise.

Failure is essential, but it is often only a step on the way to achieving your goal. Even though everything I did was extraordinarily focused and well-thought-out in advance, there were bumps in the road, literally and figuratively. Sometimes the best-laid plans had me hanging off the side of the mountain, fearing for my life. So along with goals and accepting and dealing with failure, you need to be adaptable. There are times for evaluation and times for understanding, and you need to be able to tell the difference between luck and actively taking control of your life.

LEADERBOARDS

As a habit from the days when I was working in games, I never used my name to sign support emails, unless I was answering as a manager. At Evernote, I chose the name "Allan," because I liked the way it looked in writing, and I am a fan of Edgar Allan Poe. It was always an "assumed" fact that people will respond better to technical support coming from a man, so I just became Allan and did not think anything of it.

Years later, as the team grew, we hired a diverse group of men and women around the world. We had internal leaderboards that showed how many tickets each person had in their queue, and who were our top agents on the team. We started to give out incentive prizes to top performers, in the hopes that it would spur the stragglers to do better. There was a minimal change, however.

I dug deeper. I measured how many back-and-forths replies other agents and I were sending. As many of our issues were the same and had scripted replies, they should have had the same ratio.

However, there was an alarming statistic: For every male agent we had, their touch-to-close ratio was *three times lower* than every female agent—across the board. Everyone sent out the same answers to the same problems, word for word. For some reason, on the female-named agent emails, customers were coming back and asking for clarification, asking for another solution, or often asking to be escalated to a manager.

I asked some agents if they would change their online name to an ambiguous title, like "Sam" or "Chris." After doing so, their touch-to-close ratio immediately went down—overnight.

While I had anecdotal evidence that something was wrong, I needed actual data to support my hypothesis of gender bias. By running a report on technical support agent tickets of the same number and types of questions divided split by male and female, I was able to see the difference.

These changes immediately created the potential for a 60 percent increase in efficiency for our agents by merely presenting them the opportunity to change their signature. As a side benefit, we increased morale, as the female agents who did switch it finally caught up to their male counterparts on the overall ticket leaderboard—which, in turn, kept them from leaving their positions.

OFFICER TRAINING

Like all great CEOs, Phil believed that if someone gives you a great idea, you should figure out a way to adapt it for your use. He always insisted that you give that person credit for their initial idea, but what you do with it from there is all you.

One of Phil's oldest friends was a naval submarine captain, and he spoke about him fondly and often—especially during our company All-Hands meetings. On one occasion, he told us how they had an "Official Training Program" in the Navy, where seamen who are in the officer accession process could silently observe the essential meetings with senior officers on the ship to learn as much as they could before being promoted.

He thought this idea was perfect for Evernote, especially as one of our core values was transparency. In practice, what it meant was that any employee would be allowed to join any open calendar meeting, up to 2 per month, outside their department. The theory was that it would help them to learn what was going on elsewhere in the company—or at least what questions to ask to find out.

In practice, it was not exactly how he had envisioned it. While it was true that everyone's meetings were visible, and for the most part, people were willing to add you to a meeting invite if you asked, no one had time to join more meetings than they already had on their schedule. The only people who had the opportunity to attend the meetings were interns, and since they were temporary employees, their attendance would not be the best use of their resources.

Phil decided to scrap that program and try again—after all, being adaptable is a crucial tenet of entrepreneurship. The next version was called "Evernote University." This time, instead of making people sit in other meetings that they didn't have time for and had no business sense to be in, he asked our team to come up with a list of hobbies and skills they'd be interested in learning more about off-hours.

On the list were things like Flight Training, Butchery, Foraging, and Brewing. Then we got some volunteers from the office for people who wanted to teach classes, and they received a supply budget. For classes that had no "volunteacher," Evernote would give you a specific dollar credit for a similar course elsewhere. This program was much more successful, as people were more willing to have fun with each other, learning new, non-work skills than do more work.

This success led to other non-traditional benefits added to the office. When Phil heard that people were complaining about how long it was taking them to clean on the weekends, he added a housecleaning service. When people started getting stress headaches, he brought in-office massages once a week. We already had an onsite company gym available 24/7 and a variety of snacks. When people started complaining about weight gain, we brought in a chef to cater healthy breakfast and lunch meals.

Over the years, we added an unlimited vacation policy and an additional bonus once you proved you had taken one, the option for a metro card or electric car subsidy, technology benefits, educational grants, and many other perks—but it all started with a submarine.

FINDING PURPOSE

Leon and I learned something from our years of immersion in Mexico, and it became a big part of how we do things and how we approach life.

Our first cat, Bastian, hated the boat. He hated everything about the boat, but we did not want to give up on him. We tried everything we could think of to get him to adjust, including taking him to a few veterinarians in Mexico.

We learned that life in Mexico could be vastly different from living in the States, and what we accepted as a matter of course, was the way of doing things in Mexico. We were surprised to learn that veterinarians in Mexico could not prescribe medication. They could provide primary care in their offices, like vaccines, but animals did not get cancer treatments, dialysis, cardiac care, or mood stabilizers—it simply was not done. In a country with socialized medicine, people do not spend money on animals; it was as simple as that. They could not understand our desire to put our cat on antidepressants, so we shrugged it off, figuring it was that they did not value their pets the way that we did in the States.

Then a friend of ours got sick and was taken to the hospital. When we went to visit him there, the doctor came in and wrote a prescription, and handed it to our friend, who was in bed. He obviously could not do anything with it! We were astounded.

Generally, in a hospital in the States, a nurse administers the medication that the hospital pharmacy fills from the doctors' prescriptions or orders. But in this hospital, they did not provide the drugs. Doctors gave prescriptions to patients, who were responsible for filling them and then handing over the medicine to the nurse to dispense. We thought this was very strange. If a patient did not have someone who could get the prescription filled, there would be no medication.

During our visit, my friend asked me to buy the medicine so that he could begin his course of treatment. He gave me the money, and I had to leave the hospital to procure it. I could buy the medicine at the pharmacy located across the street. I purchased the drug, returned to the hospital, and then gave him the medication. He would then give it to the nurse who was then able to administer it. I thought this was very odd, so much so that Leon and I discussed it quite a bit.

Soon after, we hired a cleaning service for our boat. The cleaning lady came with nothing in her hands, but she was willing to do anything we wanted her to do. She had preferences for what items she wanted to clean with, as long as we provided everything. We tried to give her money so she could get the specific supplies she preferred, but she would not accept it. Instead, she wrote out a shopping list for us.

Likewise, we had to provide detergent to the lady who did our laundry. She was particular about what detergent and fabric softener for us to purchase, and even had an opinion about what laundry bag we should use. We thought this was strange, but as this was their country and their culture, we felt we should adhere to it. What other choice did we have while living there? You do not move into someone else's land and revamp his or her culture.

In both cases, the women would refuse to do certain things unless we provided the supplies. Even when we offered to give the money for the items, they would not shop for them. After we had started to get enough data points on this, Leon and I came to our conclusions. The Mexican people are clear in their sense of purpose and what their responsibility is. As such, they are willing to accept responsibility for that thing, and there is no need to go further. They know what their jobs are and what they are not—the lines are clear.

With our cleaning lady, her job was to clean, and that was it. It is a housekeeper's job to direct someone to clean, cook, wash clothes, and make sure the supplies are there to do it. For the veterinarians, it was also very clearly delineated. Their job to keep animals in good health, not to use extraordinary means to prolong their life. Animals are replaceable—the Mexican culture does not anthropomorphize animals in the same way Americans do.

This culture was useful to be in while we were building up the bones of the support team since it provided us with a unique perspective on job requirements and structure. The whole structure of the country was hierarchical and bureaucratic. It was challenging for us to see how people fit into their roles because of this organization.

For people like us working for a startup company where we expected everyone to wear multiple hats, it helped us to understand the mindset of our Indian employees with whom we worked, who preferred to be and do one thing. Later, we started augmenting that team with employees in Mexico as we understood the culture there.

We were able to take the best parts of what worked in those countries and convert the culture into a model and a system that worked. It was initially difficult to comprehend for people from the startup world—where jobs are not defined—who encountered that structure. It was hard for Americans to understand the adamant refusal of people to do anything outside the defined parameters of the job simply because it was not in the job description, and it would entail taking on additional responsibilities.

The cleaning lady, the laundress, the Indian and Mexican teams viewed extraneous tasks as someone else's job and, therefore, someone else's responsibility. The idea of taking the initiative and autonomy was foreign to them. Their refusal could seem like rudeness, but I rather appreciated it because they were clear about their purpose. They knew exactly where they fit, and they became like Colin, our mechanic, experts in their particular area. We began to seek them out.

Our cleaning lady was amazing—I have never found better. She would come in and start by lifting the floorboard of the boat and drain the bilge. Then, she would scrub every inch of that boat, including the ceiling! Every time she came out, the boat would be sparkling, top to bottom, in less than two hours.

No one I have met since has ever been that good because she was clear on her purpose. As long as I had the exact brand of sponges, real Lemon Pledge, and a gallon of white vinegar, she would just plug in her headphones and sing along to whatever music she wanted to listen to that day. She knew what she was good at, and she did it.

The lady who did our laundry was incredible. She would collect all the laundry, and then she sorted it and put a little tag on everybody's wash. She had a system, and it worked.

What I learned was that when you find your purpose, be clear about it and also do not try to make people become something they are not. Do not try to question or change a culture only because it does not conform to your experiences and does not fit into your road map. If it works for them, plug yourself in, and enjoy it.

Everything we did while we were living in Mexico ended up correlating to something that we did at work or was some kind of a lesson for us. Even the time we spent at the military checkpoint gave us new perspectives on how we could make our team more efficient.

We may have held up the line briefly at the checkpoint, but we spent that time well, as we increased the level of satisfaction of the entire guard post and not just the one guard that we would usually meet. By taking 5 minutes out of our day, and 25 minutes of the guards' collective time, we may have saved hours at the checkpoint for the people who come after us. We also realized that we should spend our time at Evernote supporting not just one single person, but instead training a team and focusing on the contentment of that team. If the team were happy, the work would be more comfortable, and they would be more efficient; in turn, that would benefit the customers, which then helped the company.

We even chose our location for a specific purpose. At a startup, especially in the early days, there is no real life outside of work. Customers' moods, the quality of the builds, the reception in the media were all unpredictable. There was no way to know the number of bugs a program had, the adoption rate of the product, or the number of people who would need help at any given time. Even the things you think are under your control, such as when a new build is going to be released, or when a press release is sent out, can change at the last moment. The world of a startup is fraught with uncertainty.

So, we took charge of something that we could control; we were fortunate enough to be able to sail our boat into paradise. There was nothing better than being able to take a breath, close the laptop for a minute, walk upstairs, and look around the boat deck. I could see the Halley's Comet docked right next to us and palm trees in the distance. I knew that there were whales in the water beyond the rocks and that in only four hours, I could be in a secluded cove looking up at the stars. I could take another deep breath and be instantly transported back to our soundtrack under the stars with the waves crashing against the boat.

Sometimes people would see me as I popped above deck, and they smiled and waved at me. These people were all at peace, going about their day, but they always looked me in the eye, asked how I was doing, and genuinely wanted to know the answer. For us, it was perfect. We could not have asked for a better situation or a better group of people. Whenever I felt the stress of work starting to get to me, all I needed to do was pop my head up onto the deck for a second, look around, and I would be all right.

When you're running a business or you're starting a new enterprise, you have to be prepared to give all of yourself to the endeavor, but if you can find ways to incorporate a little bit of your non-working life into that venture, you will find that work-life balance. As Evernote started to become successful, we were able to gain the balance back that we had been missing. That certainty that we had been lacking was causing us an excessive amount of stress, but once we were on more solid footing at work, we were free to explore our other needs as well.

Once we had that certainty, we were able to help cement the culture of the company, and that was when the company itself started to sky-rocket in its success. People had been using the Evernote software, but it had not yet become a phenomenon. As soon as we dedicated time for ourselves and our well-being, the company started to benefit as well. Our customers gained from our experiences and our understanding that our happiness made us better employees and our connection to our customers strengthened the company.

FOOD

One of my favorite subjects happens to be food, which is funny to my friends as I usually choose to work through meals and, therefore, do not eat much of anything. I always tell them that my interest in food is more for the art of cooking than the act of eating, although I do enjoy delicious food. Early on in my life, I had some unique experiences with my sister when we bonded over our mutual need to feed ourselves something more flavorful and nutritious than what our mother prepared for us. She tried but could not make more than a few things well. For us to become well-adjusted kids and grow into adulthood, we needed to figure out how to fill out our diet with something that we wanted to eat, as well as being nourishing.

My sister and I would make trips to the grocery store and try to decipher the ingredients on the packaging. I remember being fascinated by the wording "processed chicken parts" on a bag of chicken nuggets. We laughed at the thought of eating beaks and eyes, but we wisely left it behind. When it came to the preparation, we would stumble around the kitchen, ignoring the warnings on the stove and the pots and pans and make whatever we wanted. I learned early on that food did not have to look pretty as long as it tasted good. And that has stuck with me ever since. You can put something that looks a mess in front of someone, and as long as it tastes good, she will be happy because you shared a part of yourself—you tried.

I call this a "Sharing Your Joy" moment. If you present something well enough with your words or with your actions, or if it comes from a place of love and your intentions are good, people will be happy with it.

We were in Mexico, surrounded by people who love food. Realistically, I know that people value food because we need it to survive, but in Mexico, people genuinely love food. They have raised the preparation and enjoyment of it to an art form. On almost every single corner, there is an ice cream parlor, and Mexican ice cream is spectacular. Their pastries are also fantastic, and the use of spices and seasoning is terrific. I have traveled around the world and have had local foods from everywhere, but I adore Mexican food, and I want to learn how to make it. There is only one problem: I do not eat red meat or pork, including any of the by-products like lard, and there is much lard in Mexican cooking.

I had to quickly learn when I was eating out how to ask for food that did not contain lard because this was an unusual request. If we were in a tourist area, the waiters, more often than not, would look askance and then try to convince me that they were serving me something without lard. Wise to this game, I generally stuck to ceviche. My theory was that you could not add lard to food that is served raw.

If we were not in a tourist area, restaurants would go to the trouble of trying to figure out how to accommodate me. The phrase for cooking without lard would be *con aceite* (with oil) or *sin manteca* (without grease), and I learned it quickly.

I also had to be careful to specify *sin cerdo* without pork. After a while, the servers in the restaurants we frequented got to know me, and they knew the kitchen might have to prepare something special to accommodate me. This idea of a special menu for me started when there was nothing on the menu they could serve me since even the rice and beans contained lard, so they created a salad out of tortilla toppings and other garnishes. They were ready for me the next time we ate there, and they created something different. These chefs seemed to view preparing their traditional food in a way that I could eat it as a challenge. As they created altered recipes, they showed me what they did, partly to prove that it did not contain any pork products or by-products, and slightly because they knew I wanted to learn how to make these things myself.

One part of Mexican cuisine that made me almost wish I ate meat was the tortillas. I do not mind corn tortillas, but since they were my only option, I began to hope that there was another choice. Flour tortillas, for the most part, are made with lard, but you make corn tortillas with oil.

There was one restaurant we visited so frequently that the servers noticed I never touched the corn tortillas. When they asked if there was a problem, I explained that I was tired of eating corn, and since I could not get flour tortillas, I would rather not eat anything. Unbeknownst to me, there was one bakery in La Paz that made flour tortillas with oil, and they were available for restaurants to purchase. As it was our habit to come to this restaurant once a week on Wednesdays, the next time we were there, they had a packet of flour tortillas for me, obviously different from their normal ones. From then on, they always had those tortillas for me whenever we visited.

There was no reason for them to go to that extra expense, other than kindness. These restauranteurs saw that I was not as happy as I could be, although for us to return to their restaurant once a week was an indication of how delicious the food was. They viewed their accommodation as an opportunity to improve. Their Contribution strengthened our Certainty in our choice of restaurant.

I am a reasonably respectable cook, and I love to recreate dishes liked by my friends and family. There was one dish, local to La Paz, that Leon and I loved, and one restaurant that made it better than any other. It was called a *molcajete* (mortar), and every part of Mexico has something called the *molcajete*. Since it refers to the cooking implement used to make it, in every place, it is different.

This difference in menus was a commonality across Mexico that caused no end of happy accidents for us. A Margarita in one place would have lime, and in another would have orange juice. A *Michelada* in one place would have lime and another Tabasco sauce. Everything was beautifully regional. The word would indicate an underlying property of the food, but there was always a local flare. The *molcajete* in Sonora was a red salsa as a small side dish, yet in La Paz, it was a soup made with grilled meat and vegetables served in a massive *molcajete*.

To make the version of the La Paz restaurant, place a *molcajete* on a hot grill for about 30 minutes until it reaches 450 degrees Fahrenheit. At the same time, grill the *nopale* cactus, flank steak, tomatoes, onions, Serrano pepper, and mushrooms. Once you cook the tomatoes, onions, and pepper, they were removed and ground into a soup with some cilantro, salt, pepper, and some other seasonings. Carefully, they would turn over the mortar and pour the mixture into the *molcajete*, and the cactus and the steak was placed over that, and the whole thing was covered with panela cheese.

We kept returning, week after week, to that restaurant. Leon could not get enough of this simple, boiling concoction. I asked them how to make it, and they told me that the key was the *molcajete* because there were minerals that came from the heated volcanic rock itself that finished the flavor. They also said that the *molcajete*s come from only one place in Mexico, which was on the mainland.

The owner showed me a catalog from a very well-known company where I could purchase them in the States. He said that the company that mines the volcanic rock makes various products and exports them worldwide while the ones sold in the local Mexican shops import them from China. He said that if we wanted one, not to purchase it from a local shop but rather let him take care of it because he had a relative who worked on the factory line. I figured that the offer was kind, but that was all I would get. What a surprise I got three months later when we had our weekly lunch, and the grinning owner presented us with three giant mortars. I was now the proud owner of 60 pounds of lava rock and had to attempt to locate a place for all of them on our boat.

In the years since, I have never made this dish because I am frankly worried about handling a 20 pound, 450-degree piece of lava rock. Leon loves that dish, but he loves me more, so I am sure he understands my reluctance.

That was the first time I asked for a recipe, and I was successful, so I began to request them from several people. People were happy to share their recipes, secret ingredients, and techniques with me. Not only did they provide written copies, but they were willing to show me how to make them. They made sure that I knew what ingredients to buy. Everyone was very particular about what it took to recreate their recipes accurately, as they had the certainty that if I used the wrong brand of flour or the wrong type of chili sauce, then it would not be correctly prepared.

I realized that the language of food was simply another way of expressing emotion. If I could cook for people, I could tap into that emotion. I started cooking food whenever someone came to visit since I like to have things ready for guests that I prepare myself, rather than merely something store-bought. If I meet somebody new, I often cook for him or her to help create a bonding experience. For my new clients, I usually bake something or offer to cook because if they see that I have taken the time, if I have opened this part of myself to them, they will understand that I do care. I have given that part of myself to them, and it is up to them to accept what I have shared physically and emotionally, but I have made a gesture that is universally understood. Of course, my friends, coworkers, and Leon especially have gained a few pounds because of the love that I have shown them in this way. The happier I am, the more I cook. I do it because I am delighted, and I want to share my joy. Leon says that people like my cooking because there is that element of love in it. Every time someone compliments me, it reminds me that cooking fills all six of my needs at once. I am uncertain every time I start something that the results will be successful. I have some small feeling of significance from people's reactions, but mostly I have a powerful sense of contribution. I am continually learning new recipes, new ways to cook, and I have a strong love for the art. But the most crucial need it fills is a certainty: I am confident in my ability, I am sure-handed, clear-headed, and I know that I will be able to tackle anything I set my mind to do.

I am now at a place where I am happy because I was able to find that work-life balance and take the time to reflect on my life. I discovered that my happiness was linked directly to my health and well-being. And as I became happier at work and in my relationships, there was a general sense of contentment in everything I did. I can share that feeling in all that I do. It follows that because I love food, I love to cook, I love to eat, and I love to share; my happiness shines through in every part of that chain. That is the place you get to when you meet all your basic needs.

If you are happy with what you do, you become better at it, and other people appreciate it. You need to take the time to be happy. No matter the perceived cost, you do need to take the time to rest, relax, and work on yourself.

FACING THE MUSIC

When you are on a boat, sound carries through the water and amplifies through the hull. It can be loud and disconcerting. If there is something noisy going on outside, sleeping becomes a losing proposition. Earplugs do not help because the boat itself begins to tremble, which in effect shakes the mast and allows the rigging to make noise above you. If you are in a thunderstorm, with heavy winds, you might as well start playing cards because there is no way to avoid the noise and the vibration. Even if you manage to tie your lines down thoroughly, you will be able to hear a boat three docks (or three miles) away, as clearly as if you were standing on it.

The summer is a time that is oppressively hot in Mexico. It gets so hot that the entire country seems deserted, and anyone visiting Baja Sur during the day in the height of the summer would think they had stumbled across an abandoned landscape. Residents work exceedingly early in the morning before the sun starts to beat down, then they disappear until much later in the day, when it begins to cool. During that oppressive heat, nothing is open, and there is nothing to do, and tourists who get lost on their way to Cabo wander around in confusion suffering from the heat.

That is not to say that there was much to do in La Paz; it was a town for resting and relaxation, not excitement. The fact that it was hot and nothing was open did not affect us because we were working all day in our air-conditioned boat. We were naturally part of the invisible daytime crowd. We did, however, sleep at night, and we did not realize that this was going off book.

During the summer nights, La Paz would come alive. One night, we started to hear loud noises around 1 A.M., and the boat began to "thump" incessantly like it was a large bass drum. We tossed and turned and covered our heads with pillows, trying our best to sleep.

The next night, again, around 1 A.M., thump, thump, thump. This time, in the distance, we could hear the faint sounds of *banda* music. We began to think that maybe it was a Mexican holiday that we did not know about, so we looked at the calendar to try to figure it out. There was no holiday indicated, so we started to ask around, but no one seemed to know anything.

The next night, at 1 A.M., it was thump, thump, thump again. After four nights of this, we were exhausted. We were zombies. I was too tired to cook, so Leon suggested that we get chicken and fries. We drove across town, and when we arrived, a sign greeted us that said, "Summer Hours: Closed until 4 P.M."

Tired and hungry, we went to the grocery store and picked up a chicken from there, then drove home. I had rested my head on the window with eyes half shut, but as we were turning into the marina, I noticed something odd. In the ordinarily empty field, there was something that looked like a circus ring. I translated the sign, and it said that this was a cockfighting event. I had never seen cockfighting, and while the cruelty repulsed part of me, part of me felt that this would be my only chance to see this in my life. I was debating with myself about how much I wanted to immerse myself in local culture versus my hatred of animal cruelty. We ultimately decided that cockfighting was not something we wanted to add to our experiences, and we turned back to the marina.

After arriving back at the boat, we discussed the possible source of the nightly noise. Now we had some evidence that something was going on, but we concluded that the ring was too small to cause all the noise. Also, it was not on the water, so that it could not have been the explanation for the thumping. We turned our sights back downtown. We decided that we would go out the next evening and find the source of the noise. We also opted to sleep during the day and work through the night because we knew we were not getting any sleep at night.

As soon as the music started, we were ready. We hopped into the truck drove downtown, toward the source of the music. We had driven this way only the day before, and everything looked normal, yet that night, we were amazed. There was a full-blown carnival in front of us! There was a band playing, and people were dancing in the streets. There were men carrying bunches of balloons. People were pushing food carts; there was even a sushi cart. I had never before seen a sushi cart anywhere, much less one in Mexico. Everyone seemed to be enjoying life, and none of this started until after midnight. This flash-mob was an almost magical occurrence. It seemed like everyone in the town was there, ready to party.

Leon and I were in awe. A stranger handed me a balloon, and someone handed Leon a bag of glitter, and suddenly everybody was screaming and throwing something in the air.

The next morning, there were no traces of previous evening's festivities anywhere. It was as if it had been all a dream. During the early hours of the morning, they hosed down the streets and washed everything away. This beautiful night carnival somehow did not exist during the day; maybe that was part of its magic. We would never have known about the nocturnal festival if we had not been willing to adapt our schedule and go out exploring. People came together to celebrate; that shared experience was a celebration of life and their joy. I have to believe this kind of thing happens elsewhere in the world.

We all still have joy in us. We want to experience things together. We want to show each other that we have something to share in a communal setting. The world needs more of that.

People sometimes ask Leon and me what was so special about our time in Mexico that makes us get lost in memories and start talking for hours; what made us love our time there so much? It was a multitude of things. I remember fondly the way they seemed to be able to turn anything into food to consume while standing. I started to understand the culture better through the food, and that transcended language.

We did not have to speak fluent Spanish. For many of the most poignant interactions we had, we did not even need to talk. We learned to communicate and connect without words. There was no time for explanations and no need.

Everything we did, everything we learned, helped us grow and connect. We found strength in each other, in our community, and were supported, loved, and happy. In turn, we were able to treat our customers at Evernote with the same love and support. It was natural and automatic to share with the people around us and online.

If you are supported, loved, and happy in your life, then you will be able to share your experiences. If you can share that security and stability within a company, you can create a positive company culture as we had at Evernote. If you can do that on a community level, you can build a community of people who support each other, whether they are on land, sea, or halfway around the world. It is possible to create a virtual online community. If we learn a little bit about each other, we can connect globally. I am sure that if we are willing to take the time to listen and learn from each other's cultures and accept each other for who we are without conditions, then the differences will not be nearly as significant as the similarities.

We can define Certainty as a firm conviction that something is the case; it has a quality of being reliably correct and a general air of confidence. It is a knowledge that affords some level of security from error. It is a mental state of living independently from doubt. To live and move in certainty is to live away from fear. It does not matter what you face, even if it is something as seemingly insignificant as food or what transportation to take, the element of fear is absent. So, choices are made with absolute certainty that we are doing the right thing. What is right is relative and different from one person to the next. In essence, if you are filled with Certainty, then you will be happy when you are following what is "right" for you.

My choices were right for me because they brought me joy, happiness, and contentment.

FINDING YOUR CENTER

Certainty is the base upon which all the other needs stand. Certainty is security; it is comfort. No matter how strong our need for Uncertainty, there will always be some desire to have peace of mind and a sense of stability. So, in life and in finding your motivating needs, you will either start or end with Certainty.

There are many healthy ways to fill our need for Certainty:

SAVE – Financial Stability is one way to fill this need. Saving money for the future can provide clarity of focus beyond the immediate present, which in turn helps you be more confident of things to come.

BUILD – Creating a structure or routine will make you feel confident in your success.

GROUP – You can fill this need by grouping things in ways that are familiar to you. It will make the world more defined as you can find the similarities among all the differences.

CONNECT – Building relationships is a wonderful way to find certainty. Connecting with friends, family, work colleagues, teammates helps you find surety.

ORGANIZE – Making sure that everything you need is available when you need it gives you a keen sense of control and certainty.

As long as you fulfill your need for Certainty, you will have the groundwork you need to take off and do amazing things.

8.
Rinse & Repeat

HASTA LA VISTA!

As Evernote grew and the product more successful, we realized that our idylls in Mexico would soon need to come to an end. Not quite ready to leave our life of vagabonding, we turned to the next best option: an RV.

As I had four years before with sailing, I now turned to learn everything I could about camping and trailers, and the overall subculture involved with living as part of the "RVer" community. I was fascinated by the similarities between "boat people" and "RV people," RV parks, and marines, but also by the differences.

For Leon and me, the transition was relatively smooth. For the littlest member of our clan, however, it was not easy.

Morgan hated it.

Every day, he would cry, relentlessly, as he had no water to swim or play in. Whenever we would drive past a mountain, he would start to shake uncontrollably, perhaps remembering our harrowing ride through the desert in Mexico.

We flipped his entire world upside down and did not give a thought to how he would take it. Honestly, we felt terrible, and it reminded us of how badly Bastian had taken to living on the boat initially.

We were such lousy pet parents.

This time, Leon refused to give Morgan up. He was determined to make Morgan learn to like the RV as much as he loved the boat.

Every night, when we would get to a new location, Leon would take Morgan out for a walk on his leash. He had let him stop and meet the other animals in the RV park, and if we were at a lake, he would let him go for a swim.

It was not long before Morgan would start bringing us his leash, begging to go out for walks. They do say that you do not own a cat, the cat owns you—Morgan was no exception to that rule.

THINGS CAN ONLY GET BETTER

Now that we had settled into RV life, we were untethered. We began to wander across the country, parking randomly at major airport hubs whenever we needed to return to one of the Evernote offices to put out a fire or show up for an in-person meeting.

One day, as I was researching an answer for one of our customers, I noticed that one of my favorite musicians was playing a concert in Orlando, Florida, at Disney World.

This musician rarely gave live performances, and this would be a special occasion for me because I had never seen him perform live. The concert was four days from then, and we were roughly four days' drive from Orlando.

"So, um, Leon," I began.

"Huh, what?" He replied, a typical response while he was driving.

"Howard Jones is playing at Disney World," I said.

"Oh. Cool."

"Can we go?"

"Sure, yeah."

"Great! It's in four days."

He looked over at me with one of those withering looks that every long-married couple understands. It was a calculation to determine exactly how serious I was and what this was going to cost him to turn me down.

Whatever he saw in my face, he decided that it was not worth arguing.

What I had discovered was that Disney World had an RV park called Fort Wilderness—inside the park—and that they had long-term spots available. As Orlando was a major airport, we would be able to reach all of the Evernote offices quickly whenever needed, so we cobbled together a plan. We had chosen to live in La Paz because the name meant "Peace," and the town was peaceful. It gave us the strength we needed to get all the things we needed to do. Similarly, Disney World is the Happiest Place on Earth. We were heading straight for it. We could now live there *for as long as we wanted*.

For the next four days, we drove furiously across the country.

We would control our fate once again.

It was the perfect plan.

Three days and 2500 miles later, we reached Florida. We had been driving almost nonstop, sleeping in truck stops to save time. Suddenly, we heard a loud "bang," and the RV started to shake violently.

Smoke coming from the passenger side.

A few minutes later, there was another loud bang.

We rolled slowly into a conveniently located rest area and found that we had blown three tires out of our RV's six and that the brakes had locked. It was too late to get them repaired that evening, so we had to sleep in the rest area that night and wait until the morning.

Leon was furious.

He complained that this was a terrible idea, we should not have done this, it was too expensive, and everything that could have possibly gone wrong just did—why didn't we just stay in one place? He was only saying obvious things, but it started to show me he was getting tired of the life of travel he had once wanted.

We had gone from such a place of certainty, and now we started to spiral back down into uncertainty. Life is like that—you have to be tending to things constantly. If you get complacent, you can lose everything you had.

FORT WILDERNESS

The next day, after repairing the RV, we continued to Disney World. We checked into our spot in Fort Wilderness, and when they asked us for our checkout date, we left it open.

After pulling into our spot, I took a deep breath. Evernote was at a crucial point: We had expanded to nine countries, and Leon and I were traveling to the various offices at least once a month to train someone, fix something, or just be around for meetings. We had just had four days of tension driving across the country, ending with one of our worst fights ever—and we were now barely on speaking terms.

I looked at the map the check-in attendant handed us and noticed there were daily activities. One of them was a daily "Chip and Dale Campfire Sing-Along." The Howard Jones Concert was not until the next day, and we were tired, but I suggested to Leon that we get out of the RV and at least walk around.

"What would you say to getting some s'mores?" I asked.

He looked at me like I had three heads. It may have been the question, or probably that the first thing I had chosen to say to him in two days that did not have to do with work was so ridiculous.

"What did you say?" he asked.

"Well, there's this campfire thing, over here. It says there are free hot cocoa and s'mores," I said, pointing at the map.

He continued to look at me like I was talking another language. "You realize it's like 90 degrees out, right? And 85% humidity?"

Perhaps because of his attitude, or maybe from cabin fever, I doubled down. "I think it will be fun. I am going to go. You can stay here if you want."

Within a few minutes, I was out the door, walking toward the meeting site. As Leon had mentioned, it was 90 degrees and very humid, and I was heading to a large campfire—which produced more heat. It certainly was not one of my better ideas, but I was committed to it.

When I arrived, there were a bunch of other campers in various stages of heatstroke—all looking like they had made a poor life choice. Until that is, Chip and Dale arrived. At that point, everyone forgot what they were personally feeling. All thoughts of heat, misery, fighting, and work disappeared—we all just got lost in the magic of these cartoon chipmunks. They sang, they danced—we joined in, clapping and laughing. We ate many s'mores and drank hot chocolate, despite the heat outside.

At one point during the festivities, Leon joined me. I turned to him, and he gave me a look that told me that he was going to move forward from the tense past few days. He took a bite of my s'more and joined in as we all started singing *Supercalifragilisticexpialidocious*.

I noticed that Chip and Dale's costumes had air-conditioning units built-in, and I later saw that there were similar fan and mister systems around the campfire to keep everyone else cool—but on that first night, none of that mattered.

We ended up staying at Fort Wilderness many months, immersing ourselves in the certainty of having the Happiest Place on Earth during some of the most tumultuous times of Evernote and our relationship.

DISNEY MAGIC

It may surprise you to hear this, but one of the benefits of living on the grounds of Disney World is that you are, in all actuality, residing within a Disney park. There are morning wakeup calls from Mickey Mouse, evening fireworks, the aforementioned Chip and Dale campfires—and of course, the parks.

One of our first orders of business was to get Annual passes so that we could enter any park on the property whenever we wanted. As we were also "residents" of the property, we could make use of what they called "Magic Hours" and enter early or stay later—depending on the park hours that day.

As the stresses of Evernote began to pile on, we found that more of an escape was needed. The tension was building again between Leon and me as we would argue over the different ways to run our respective departments and manage our employees. I frequently found myself grabbing my laptop and hopping the boat over to the Magic Kingdom, where I would sit in a cafe at the top of Main Street and sip coffee while answering emails.

On some especially crazy days, I would forgo the laptop and pop over to ride Pirates of the Caribbean or Space Mountain once or twice, then return—rejuvenated to continue with the day.

My favorite pastime of all, however, was to head over to EPCOT's World Showcase and sit in the cafe in their recreation of Paris. At the same time, I would do my weekly status updates or take my calls from a quiet corner in the back of the Canada pavilion. When I was feeling run-down, I would walk the streets of Morocco and dream about visiting one day, stop and listen to the classical pop group Nova Era in the Italy Pavilion, and watch the Chinese Acrobats. Before leaving EPCOT, I would ride Spaceship Earth, and let Jeremy Irons' incredible narration spur my imagination, and renew my motivation to work on changing the world.

While we had initially come there on a whim, each day we stayed was eye-opening. The perfection that Disney requires, the attention to detail for every customer, the "magic" it creates—I was a sponge, learning everything I could, and incorporating it back into my work. You create from your environment; my environment was so vibrant and joyful; I could not help but pour all of that magic to our customers.

FANS

By now, Leon and I were frequently traveling to the offices around the world—we were on a bi-monthly rotation between Zurich, Austin, Mexico, and San Francisco and wherever our "home base" happened to be—and we would often split trips to build in more face-time.

As always, in-office weeks were minimally productive, filled as they were with executive and vendor meetings as well as team reviews—and just general chit-chat. We saved the "real work" for back at the hotel, where we needed to answer the mountains of escalations and write new training materials. After two weeks of ten hours of work in the office, followed by eight hours more at my hotel, I was exhausted, frustrated, and just a tiny bit cranky. I was looking forward to returning to my home to Disney World so that I could relax again immersed in the glow of Disney and get back to a regular schedule.

As I was settling into my First-Class seat, looking out the window and sipping my pre-flight cocktail, a kindly gentleman sits down next to me and asks, "Oh, do you work for Evernote?"

I looked down, and I was wearing one of my Evernote T-Shirts. Confident that my years of working in customer-facing positions hid the rage I was feeling, I silently swore under my breath before replying, with my best customer service demeanor:

"Why, yes, I do! I happen to be the global head of tech support."

"Oh, that's great! I'm having a bit of trouble with . . ."

I was silently seething. This thing that I used to love with abandon had now become a burden. All I wanted to do was have a 5-hour flight to myself, to rest and relax before getting back to work, and yet my success trapped me.

We spoke for around 20 minutes as I patiently walked him through the things that Evernote was and was not, the things it could and could not do, and I took down the notes and suggestions he had on usability. I promised I would file them after we land and let him know when we had an update.

Confident that I had done my duty as Evernote's top evangelist, I settled back into my seat.

FIREWORKS

In the years following, we spent many nights driving the highways of America. I would have my laptop firmly anchored to me in the passenger seat, Morgan would be seated between us, and Leon would be looking out into the distance, pondering our strange existence.

One typical night, as we were driving, exhausted, on a two-lane highway, through an otherwise nondescript town, we saw fireworks ahead in the distance. It was likely for us to have lost track of days, so we checked to see if it was a holiday—which it was not.

We continued to drive, and again, we saw fireworks.

Curiosity had now set in—what was the purpose of these fireworks? And from where were they coming?

Onward we drove, on this desolate, lonely road, for another hour. More and more fireworks were set off into the sky ahead of us—and it seemed, at least, to us, this beautiful show was just for us. We settled in and began to appreciate it, smiling with each new blast.

We were drawn to the source like moths to a flame. For miles we drove, following these fireworks. It turned out to be a lone man, in a dirt lot, shooting them off one by one. Our curiosity got the better of us, and we pulled to the side of the road, then approached him. I was curious to know his motivation.

He told us, "seeing fireworks make people happy. I'm doing my part to change the world."

Was that our purpose as well? I was not sure anymore.

VALUES

In February 2013, on a Friday afternoon, I got the call I had never hoped to receive.

Evernote's security was compromised.

What little information we had was not looking good—while there was evidence of an outside incursion into our system, we did not know the extent or intent of the breach.

We had to act fast.

Within hours, I had my team activated, prepared to begin handling an emergency. We started updating our playbook and running our scenarios, trying to write procedures for an event we had not fully anticipated. We had team members all over the world, translating messages ready to go out as soon as our legal team was willing to release announcements.

Additionally, we had other team members preparing to train employees for the inevitable backlog that we expected was coming.

On Saturday morning, we reset 50 million user account passwords.

On Monday morning, we had received 20,000 support emails.

By Tuesday, that number was up to 35,000, and we were receiving additional 15,000-20,000 emails per day.

By Wednesday, we had trained all 450 employees of Evernote to answer support.

By Friday, the number of standing messages was at 20,000 and holding.

While this was no mean feat, and certainly cause for celebration, the mood in the company was overwhelmingly somber. A security breach was a sobering experience, but this went beyond what one might have expected. There was a natural explanation for this to those who understood the culture at Evernote. For years, the promise to customers had been three-fold:

- YOUR DATA IS PRIVATE.
- YOUR DATA IS PORTABLE.
- YOUR DATA IS PROTECTED.

Every employee used this as a mantra, and it ran through our veins, like blood. Every product, every release, everything we did, was designed to those core values. We had failed in our promises. How could we possibly come back from that?

TURNTABLES

In the weeks following the breach, I was in the office nonstop. One morning, as walked among the support team, I noticed that the employees were focused intently, headphones firmly in place, mouthing words silently while powering through answering their emails. Before, the department had been a place of conversation and laughter; now, people quietly sang along with their playlists.

I made a quick decision.

I asked every person currently working on support to load their playlists into a joint playlist, for everyone to hear. This way, we would be joined together, rather than siloed from each other. As more people joined in from around the world, we started adding in more songs to the list. Soon we had a list of thousands of songs, playing on shuffle, with songs from Japan, Korea, Russia, Singapore, America, Mexico, Germany, France, England—everywhere we had employees, we had music. Different musical styles and tastes. Johnnie Cash would be followed by Queen, then by Gwar, with a little bit of K-Pop thrown in.

It was glorious.

I noticed something else; when we started, the music selections were as dark and somber as the company mood. By the end of the third day, there were some happier songs in the mix. After the end of a week, the playlist was more cheerful, and the mood among the team was upbeat as well.

We had given each other a communal boost.

STOICISM

A month after the breach, things had started to return to a new normal. Leon and I were considering returning to the RV shortly, but still had daily meetings with the legal team, and we were also working on a transition to a new support tool to handle the higher volume of support cases we now had regularly. As we were facing our highest amount of support requests ever, the race was on to complete the database transfer.

One morning, while only walking into the office, I tripped on a cobblestone, fell, and broke my foot. It was the type of pain that brings instant tears, even with the shock. I tried to stand and found that I could not. My cell phone was locked in my hand with a death grip, so I dialed Leon for help. He was already upstairs for his morning team briefing, and he and another colleague rushed downstairs right away. The two hoisted me into the backseat of our car and whisked me off to the hospital.

It was extremely inconvenient timing. The transition was not complete to the new system. The company was still at a sort of precarious state from the breach a month prior—I could not figuratively "go down" and leave them.

I made a choice. I would get through the healing process without any medicine or anything to cloud my ability to think. I would be there for the team and would not let this little injury stop me. No painkillers. No herbal remedies. Nothing but ice packs and heating pads and that awful boot while my bones knit back together.

I—politely—badgered the trauma nurses to get me through the ER quickly so I could make it back to the office as soon as possible. Within two hours of the whole incident, I was at the office, which meant I only missed one meeting. Unfortunately, I did not think far enough ahead. I could not carry my laptop with crutches, and I did not have a backpack with me. I needed help getting to the conference room.

A curious side effect of this that I had not anticipated was that when your body is in a constant pain state is that it does not sleep, and you are in a heightened state of awareness. I managed to finish the database transition sooner than expected.

Something else I learned is that bravery and stupidity look remarkably similar to outside observers. It would have been too easy at any point for me to give in and take the painkillers, but I would have been abandoning a fantastic group of people who were already struggling to come back from their lowest point.

When you are a leader, you need to model the behavior you want your team to have. I made it very clear throughout that entire experience that I neither wanted nor expected people to have anything like my work ethic. I explained that it was unhealthy, and if this had happened at any other time, I would have gladly taken a vacation and bed rest. I wanted them to know that they could count on me, though, no matter how terrible things got at the company. People need leaders. They need people to look up to and emulate. The trouble is, through my overworked, sleep-deprived, pain-addled brain, the behavior I was modeling was not entirely what I thought it was.

PARALYSIS

Having been at the company from the beginning, I began to sense when it was time to move on. As an entrepreneur and a vagabond, I had the yearning to travel once more, and I had started spending entirely too much time tied to the offices. What would be the dream job for many was beginning to be stifling to me. It was amazing to see everything that I had built become so loved and integral by so many people, but there was something very wrong with me.

One morning, as I was walking to my desk, I felt a sharp pain in my side. I tried to ignore it, but the pain grew strong, and it became hard to ignore. I walked to the elevator to take me down to the first-floor cafeteria, and, while alone in the elevator, I collapsed, in tears, partly from the pain but mostly from the exhaustion.

There I was, alone, sobbing on the floor of that elevator. I am unsure how long I had been there, but when the elevator reached the first floor, it opened to Phil. He saw me there, crying, crumpled in a ball, unable to move. He picked me up slowly, supported me, and we went for a walk outside.

We walked in silence for a bit, as I calmed down. When I was ready, Phil asked, "What's up?"

"I'm not happy."

"Obviously," He replied.

I remained mostly quiet as we continued to walk up the block. As I started to stammer out an apology for taking up valuable CEO time, he became agitated. He turned me to face him and had me look him right in the eyes.

He said, "You know, none of this stuff matters—what other people say, what *they* want—none of it. You cannot let it affect you personally. Roll it off."

I was not receptive at all. It was as if Phil was speaking to a brick wall.

I needed to leave the office. It was time to go home—but after all my years on the road, did I even have one?

HAIL AND FAREWELL

We had driven the RV to Las Vegas, where it was only a quick flight to the office—and only an eight-hour drive in an emergency. We had started house hunting there because of the favorable tax rate, and the friendly community seemed like as good a place as any to settle down. With the boat up in Redwood City across from Evernote Headquarters, I decided to go to Vegas to rest up.

A few days after flying there, the pain returned, and worse. Leon was away on a month-long business trip for Evernote, but my friend Christina was there and urged me to go to the doctor. When I told her I already had an appointment, she insisted that I keep it instead of making another or go to an urgent care like I had been doing—and would not take no for an answer.

Two hours later, we were sitting in the doctor's office. He was asking me questions that embarrassed me into a stunned silence. Thankfully, my observant friend was able to speak for me. In an almost out-of-body experience, I watched as Christina and the doctor discussed my condition.

"How long has she been like this?" he asked.

Without hesitation, Christina replied, "At least three months. She has lost a lot of weight—her face is much thinner than when we first met. Her hair is coming out in large clumps when she brushes it. And she never sleeps."

At that point, the doctor pushed on my abdomen. My whole body jerked.

"See? She's been like that for months, but she'll tell you she's fine."

In no time, I had a diagnosis of a tumor completely blocking my intestinal tract. The very next morning, I was scheduling surgery to have it removed, with her at my side.

While I was preparing for surgery, Christina gave me a penetrating stare. "I know you say you love what you do, but your body says otherwise. You are running yourself ragged. I will never tell you what to do, but I think you realize you need to make a change."

When I came out of surgery, I messaged Phil and told him I wanted to work out how to transition out of the company.

In the spring of 2014, I closed the Evernote chapter of my life to move on and start my next company. I told the team with the following letter:

Ave Atque Vale.

In the past six years, Evernote has grown exponentially.

When I joined the team, you could count the number of full-time employees on your fingers. We had less than half a million users. We were located in a mostly forgotten office in Sunnyvale, CA, and most of the customers (and press) still called it EverNote.

A lot has changed—it turned into a global company with over 100 million users, with offices worldwide, hundreds of employees, speaking (at least) 9 different languages, and multiple product lines—including actual physical goods.

(When I first got the call asking me to come work for Evernote back in 2008, I can honestly tell you I didn't think we'd ever be selling backpacks and water bottles!)

On May 15th, 1905, Las Vegas, Nevada, was founded. It is therefore fitting that on May 15th, 2014, I am leaving Evernote to start a new journey and to help shape the culture of that city.

I'm honored to have known and worked with you all. I wish everyone here continued success.

9.
Epilogue

MOTIVATIONS

The initial motivation for authoring a book based on my experiences to teach these concepts came from other people who urged me to write it down because my story resonated with them. My different experiences make me unique, and that is always surprising to me. What is even more amazing, though, is that I did not even realize that I was hitting the necessary basic needs for success since all I have ever done is to put my thoughts into action.

People who learned of our journey were fascinated that we took off to live on a sailboat in Mexico. They found it remarkable that we were able to pursue the Silicon Valley startup dream while residing outside of the country. And that is fine—it *is* different. But here is the thing, although following my desire to be part of a startup and living my idea of a fairy-tale lifestyle was particularly important to me, my relationships *meant more*.

That is the thing that no one teaches you in business books. You get frameworks, and you will learn steps to get to 10x, 100x growth if you try hard enough. But they do not show you the other side—the bit where you can barely hold it together because you have given everything you can to succeed. Where your friends, family, and life falls apart because you neglect them entirely.

There is the real secret to success—it is creating and maintaining the bonds where you find your most significant source of strength. They are what will be there through the whole cycle, from uncertainty to certainty and back again. Those relationships mean more to me than any company *ever* will—even one that has become a part of the lives of millions of people every day.

A RISKY DECISION

After Leon and I had been living in Mexico for a year and a half, an acquaintance of mine asked if he could visit us as he had saved some money and wanted to travel somewhere, and he did not have a particular destination in mind. We had talked about how peaceful things were in La Paz, and how relaxing and undemanding life was there. It was the sort of trip he was looking for, so he decided to take the chance and come.

There were a few things that were immediately unusual about this request and our offer. While I had known Andrew for ten years, I had never met him in person. Yet, both Leon and I were perfectly fine with inviting him to share our small living space for a week. What was even more incredible was that Andrew took the risk to come to stay with two strangers in a country he knew little about and where he did not speak the language.

So, after some minor planning, Andrew showed up at the bus station in the middle of town. I spotted him right away and picked him up. Leon and I did not change our routine and spent a typical week at work.

Andrew relaxed, hung out, used the Jet Ski, and generally chilled out. During that week, we would chat, laugh, and he would go out exploring, but he frequently observed how Leon and I were living, working together, and enjoying life.

What he told us was that visiting us was the first risky or impulsive vacation he had ever taken, and he learned something vital. He discovered that he could simply enjoy being by himself and did not need lots of activities or several people to visit when he took vacation time. It did open up his world to the fact that he had missed out on all sorts of experiences by staying at home in his comfort zone.

After the week was over, Andrew flew back home to the States and then emailed me within a few weeks to let me know he had made a decision: he was going to follow our lead and move to Poland without even learning the language first. He wanted our input on what he needed to do to achieve this goal.

Within a year, he was living in Poland, married to a woman who enjoys making risky decisions with him, and has a daughter who is the center of his universe.

10.
Now What?

RECAP

The first step on your journey of self-discovery is to figure out where you are with your individual needs. The simple assessment that follows will help you discover what your needs are currently. Take this test periodically to find out how you are progressing and how you are filling your needs as they change over time.

At the end of each chapter on basic human needs, there are some ideas on how to fulfill them to help you manage your life. As an additional exercise, write down what you do during each day of a typical week. See if the things you do match what your needs are "asking" of you. If not, try making some slight changes where you can. Small adjustments do make an enormous difference.

The test has no "right" answers, and everyone's "score" will be different. Your needs are just that—yours. As you go through life, those needs and requirements may fluctuate, and you might find that your needs and priorities have changed.

Read each question and think carefully about how it applies to you right now. On a separate piece of paper, write down the question number and your response of "Yes," "No," or "Partly" for each question.

The need you have scored highest in is your driving need. Your second highest score would be your secondary motivator unless you had two tied for the top spot. All the others are your supporting needs in order of importance to you at this time in your life. To be the happiest, most successful version of you, you need to be filling those needs in those proportions.

I wish you well on your journey!

ASSESSMENT

1. When the phone rings, I rush to answer it.
2. When I find things I like, I tend to think of how good life would be if I had it.
3. Visionaries and theorists fascinate me.
4. There is always something new to be learned.
5. Sometimes the most critical work is not what pays you.
6. Prestige is crucial to me.
7. Other people are impressed by me.
8. Meeting new people is exciting.
9. It is vital to contribute to my community.
10. It is important to be forgiving and merciful.
11. If I must disappoint someone, I am usually warm and caring.
12. I am a leader.
13. I would rather be too critical than indifferent.
14. I worry about what people are saying about me.
15. I value tradition.
16. I value harmonious relationships.
17. I value discourse over agreement.
18. I value consistent thinking.
19. I value a vivid imagination.
20. I understand the value of others.

21. I understand people using instinct.
22. I think about the future.
23. I tend to be interested in the possibility of things.
24. I take pride in who I am.
25. I speak in generalities.
26. I prefer writers who use analogies, metaphors, and symbolism.
27. I prefer writers who say what they mean.
28. I prefer making decisions.
29. I prefer a contract to begin work.
30. I need fulfillment.
31. I make decisions somewhat casually.
32. I like working under a deadline.
33. I like to learn to teach what I learn.
34. I like to evaluate myself.
35. I like making a difference.
36. I have many acquaintances.
37. I have deep friendships.
38. I have an opinion on most issues.
39. I hate being bored.
40. I enjoy working on projects.
41. I enjoy research and development.
42. I enjoy being an example to others.
43. I embrace change.
44. I always aspire to improve.
45. I chat with others while standing in line.
46. I believe in giving back.
47. I approach people personally and casually.
48. I am serious and determined.
49. Emotions rule me.
50. I am regularly on time or early.
51. I am regularly late.
52. I am realistic.
53. I am organized.
54. I am open to change.

55. I am imaginative.
56. I am idealistic.
57. I am an outgoing person.
58. I am an emotional person.
59. I am a logical person.
60. I am a competitive person.
61. Facts have apparent meanings.
62. Facts are useful for explaining situations.
63. Common sense is rarely questionable.
64. Children do not use their imaginations enough.
65. Adaptation is more important than organization.
66. Failure is not a failure if you keep trying.

SCORING

For every "Yes," give yourself 1 point. For every "No," give yourself 0 points, and for every "Partly," give yourself half a point. The questions correlate to each need as follows:

CERTAINTY: 15, 18, 27, 29, 32, 48, 50, 52, 53, 61, 63

UNCERTAINTY: 8, 19, 22, 23, 25, 31, 43, 51, 54, 55, 56

SIGNIFICANCE: 2, 6, 7, 14, 24, 28, 34, 38, 39, 57, 60

LOVE/CONNECTION: 1, 10, 11, 13, 16, 21, 37, 45, 47, 49, 58

GROWTH: 3, 4, 26, 40, 41, 44, 59, 62, 64, 65, 66

CONTRIBUTION: 5, 9, 12, 17, 20, 30, 33, 35, 36, 42, 46

Acknowledgments

I N THE same way that my journey has been shaped by my experiences, so has this book been formed by the people who have influenced it along the way.

To my parents—Chuck and Pam Richardson, who without their belief in me and financial support at key times, I would not have been able to have had the education or luxury to achieve many of the things I talk about in this book. And to my birth mother, Susan, who gave me a love of constantly learning and encouraged my writing.

To Mark Rowland, who was the first to casually suggest that these stories I kept bringing up in mentor sessions might make a "good book for entrepreneurs." Thanks also to Mark for getting me trained as a coach and introducing me to behavioral psychology, so I have some clue what I am talking about.

To Phil Libin, Andrew McGeachie, Brandon Volbright, Dmitry Stavisky, Alex Pachikov, Pete Kvitek, Dave Engberg, and of course, Stephan Pachikov—and all the other CoreStreeters and Evernoters who helped me make the world better for so many years.

To Della Rucker, for agreeing to read, proofread, and be a sounding board for this book while waiting in the intense Austin, Texas heat to see Jimmy Kimmel Live—and still doing it even after she cooled down.

To Christina Aldan, for saving my life back then, and being there for me every day since so that I would be here to keep changing the world.

To Cleveland McLeish, who helped me figure out the best order to get this on paper—and had the patience to listen and transcribe my incessant audio notes in Evernote until we figured out a framework I could work with on my own.

To all the people who have read this book in its unfinished form and given me the feedback and suggestions that made it better, especially Dylan Jorgenson, Brad Jones, and Lauren Koenig. They all asked me, in their own ways, to go deeper.

To Larry Hitchcock, CEO of Socialeads, one of the most adaptable serial entrepreneurs I've ever encountered. Thank you, Larry, for being so supportive of me and all the other entrepreneurs you meet.

To Lee Constantine and Publishizer, who supported me through all my middle-of-the-night manifestos and musings until we found the perfect fit.

To the whole team at Sunbury Press, and my editor, Abigail Henson, who fixed all my rookie mistakes.

To all the entrepreneurs and innovators who are reading this—no matter where you are on your journey, I am thankful that you picked this book up and carried it along on your path for a bit.

And finally, to Leon Wilde, who joined me for every step of this journey and taught me that there is more to life than just work.

About the Author

HEATHER WILDE was the eighth employee of Evernote, where she oversaw the company's growth from thousands to 100 million customers. She has published popular games, worked with the United States DoD, Navy, Air Force, and Space Force, trained Fortune 500 brands, advised hundreds of startups, and managed major multinational nonprofit programs. At her own nonprofit, Serenze Global, and as a fractional CTO through her company ROCeteer, her award-winning work keeps the "Unicorn Whisperer" constantly traveling across the globe to find the next unicorn.

She happily resides in Las Vegas, Nevada.

CPSIA information can be obtained
at www.ICGtesting.com
Printed in the USA
BVHW030339241120
593917BV00010BA/27/J

9 781620 063347